Changing Course

**Blueprint for Peace in Central America
and the Caribbean**

PACCA

**Institute for Policy Studies
Washington, D.C.**

The Institute for Policy Studies is a nonpartisan
research institute. The views expressed in this
study are solely those of the drafters.

Published by the Institute for Policy Studies.

Copies of this book are available from the Institute for Policy Studies, 1901 Q Street, N.W.,
Washington, D.C. 20009; from the Central America Resource Center, P.O. Box 2327, Austin, TX
78768; and from Food First Books, 1885 Mission
Street, San Francisco, CA 94103.

First Printing, 1984
Second Printing, 1984
ISBN 0-89758-037-0

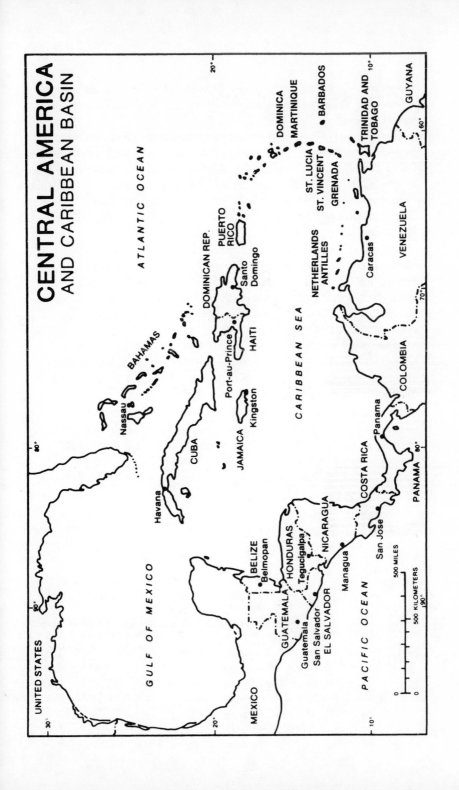

CENTRAL AMERICA
AND CARIBBEAN BASIN

Introduction

The true American goes not abroad in search of monsters to
destroy . . . [America] well knows that by once enlisting under
other banners than her own, were they even the banners of foreign independence, she would involve herself, beyond the
power of extrication, in all the wars of interest and intrigue, of
individual avarice, envy, and ambition. She might become the
dictatress of the world; she would no longer be the ruler of her
own spirit.

John Quincy Adams
July 4, 1821

As this report is written, the United States has some 15,000 troops in
Central America and the Caribbean; U.S. warships patrol off the coasts
of Nicaragua; military exercises in Honduras occasion continuing deployment of U.S. troops and the development of a complex of military
facilities in that country. The Central Intelligence Agency is funding a
multimillion dollar covert military campaign against Nicaragua, launched
from bases in Honduras and Costa Rica. The Administration has committed itself to a regime in El Salvador that faces a determined guerrilla
force composed of left and center elements and a popular resistance led
by important church officials. So deep is the Reagan investment in
preventing a left victory in El Salvador, that the prospect of that
government's collapse could well trigger direct U.S. military intervention.

The failure of current Central America policy is rooted in its premises.
The Administration assumes that social revolutions in the region must
be seen as an expression of Soviet global ambitions. "The national

security of all the Americas is at stake," President Reagan warned a joint session of Congress, adding more ominously, "who among us would wish to bear responsibility for failing to meet our shared obligation?"[1]

By invoking national security and focusing on global implications, U.S. policy makers have obscured the roots and distorted the nature of local conflicts. Within the Reagan administration, crisis managers have replaced diplomats knowledgeable about the area's history and culture.[2] Military intelligence reports take precedence over seasoned political advice. Policy discussions are reduced to arguments over tactics and solutions that are often framed in military terms.

The Administration has tried to narrow the public debate to the issue of national security, even as opposition builds against its policies. By squeezing the complex range of U.S. interests in Central America into a cold war framework the president has been able to intimidate legislators and make them reluctant to take the political risk of challenging the policy directly. Growing public opposition is seen as an obstacle to be managed by high-sounding rhetoric and unfulfillable promises. Secrecy, exaggeration and outright distortion are enlisted in the effort to gain support. The conclusions of the Report of the National Bipartisan Commission headed by former Secretary of State Henry Kissinger hinge upon the gravity of the Soviet threat to U.S. national security in Central America. But the real crisis is in the inability of the United States to respond appropriately to profound changes in Central America which this nation cannot prevent without damaging our own democratic institutions, our economy and our national security.

The failure to assess the true character of U.S. interests in the region and the real choices that lie before us has led to the crisis. U.S. prestige has been invested in a barbarous Salvadoran regime, dependent upon external U.S. aid and internal death squads. An alarming escalation of U.S. military and financial commitments is proceeding without a congressional or public debate about the actual interests at stake. The Administration's Central America policy has generated political polarization within the United States and growing misgivings among allies in Europe and in the hemisphere about the prudence of U.S. leadership.

As a result, the policy choices open to the United States are being dangerously constricted. Administration spokesmen suggest that too much has already been invested in El Salvador for the United States to withdraw. Soon, the choice may be symbolic defeat or direct U.S. intervention.

This report is written in the belief that it is not too late to change our course. The upheaval in Central America need not become a tragedy for U.S. policy, but rather it can serve to compel a re-examination of what relationship the United States should have to the region as we prepare to enter the twenty-first century. An alternative policy must begin with a full debate aimed at making a sensible assessment of developments in the region and U.S. interests there.

The invocation of the magic words "national security" can turn virtually any region in the world into a "threat." Even tiny Grenada, an island slightly larger than Martha's Vineyard, with fewer than 110,000 inhabitants, became a national security threat requiring an invasion that alarmed most of the nations of Latin America. A sensible definition of national security should enable us to distinguish the vital from the peripheral, the enduring from the temporary. It must focus on our *fundamental* security requirement: the ability to secure our own social experiment at home and pursue it free from external threat. Successful revolutions in Central America—in and of themselves—cannot threaten U.S. security. Such revolutions can be insulated from the U.S.–Soviet competition. This should be a prime objective of U.S. foreign policy.

Revolutions are traumatic, costly social eruptions, whose outcomes are difficult to predict. In Central America, revolutionary governments are almost certain to be nationalist in their inspiration, prickly in their independence, and, given the history of U.S. activities in the region, suspicious, if not hostile, towards the United States. Their attempts to redistribute the resources of their countries more equitably are likely to produce a variety of socialist or mixed economies.

The revolutions in Nicaragua, El Salvador and Guatemala are rooted in poverty and political repression. In each country, the economic system has been dominated for generations by a wealthy few, securing their privilege through military repression. During the first 30 years of this century, repeated U.S. interventions helped protect that order against periodic social revolts.

After World War II, economic growth created modern sectors in the economies of Central America but did not alter the entrenched system of inequality. Reform efforts led by a growing middle class were squelched. The United States supported democratic reform rhetorically, but fear of revolution left U.S. policy hostage to the very dictators or oligarchies that blocked all avenues to change save violent revolution. What we face today in Central America is not the product of external design: it is the legacy of that system and of our own prior policies.

The revolutions in Central America have been long in the making, indeed long expected. They are not the products of a Soviet–Cuban conspiracy, although many of their leaders are inspired by Castro's defiance of the United States.

Successful revolutions need not threaten the United States; they need not lead to governments that are dependent upon the Soviet Union. Every nationalist government of the left in the Western hemisphere desires to do business with and receive aid from all regions of the world, including the United States and the Soviet Union. Nicaragua, for example, currently sustains a mixed economy and a political model far different from that of the Soviet Union or Cuba. The Nicaraguan government seeks aid and trade around the world, most of which comes from non-communist countries in Western Europe and the hemisphere. Less than 20 percent of Nicaragua's trade is with the Soviet Union and Eastern Europe, despite U.S. efforts to isolate Nicaragua economically from the West.[3]

Administration spokesmen have elevated Central America's importance to U.S. security, and insist that the United States is being tested there. The struggle is portrayed as a symbol, a demonstration of U.S. credibility to its allies. "If we cannot defend ourselves there," President Reagan warned the Congress, "we cannot expect to prevail elsewhere. Our credibility would collapse; our alliances would crumble, and the safety of our homeland would be put in jeopardy."[4]

This argument, reminiscent of the rationale used to defend U.S. intervention in Vietnam, does not square with the facts. Allies in Europe and in the hemisphere express doubts about U.S. policy and oppose U.S. military intervention. Their concern is not whether the United States has the will to use the military force at its disposal, but whether its leaders have the prudence and judgment to deploy that force wisely. Disproportionate commitment in support of disreputable regimes fighting their own people will hardly build that confidence.

National revolutions have already transformed the global map in the years since World War II and will continue to do so. No matter what happens in Central America, we are likely to face revolutionary ferment in Pakistan, the Philippines, South Korea and elsewhere. Will support for those regimes also become a test of U.S. resolve? The cost of opposing popular revolutions around the world exceeds our resources. Central America, exactly because our power in the region is greater than almost anywhere else, is the place to begin to forge a more constructive policy response.

We are and will remain the dominant force in the Caribbean and

15

Central America. No one can challenge that reality. The problem we face is how to exercise that power in accordance with real U.S. interests.

An alternative path was suggested by Franklin Delano Roosevelt's response to the Mexican nationalization of U.S. oil companies in 1938. Then, as now, influential voices were raised calling for military intervention. The Mexican government was branded "bolshevik" and "red." U.S. credibility was said to be at stake. If the Mexicans were allowed to get away with this act, it was argued, U.S. property would be at risk everywhere.

Roosevelt balked at military intervention, which would have undermined the "good neighbor" policy he had declared towards nations in the region. Instead, the United States maintained diplomatic relations with Mexico and entered into negotiations regarding compensation for the oil companies. When three years later, the United States entered World War II, Mexico and most of Latin America aided the Allied powers.

Henry Kissinger has defined Central America as a test case: "If we cannot manage in Central America, it will be impossible to convince threatened nations in the Persian Gulf and in other places that we know how to manage the global equilibrium."[5] We agree that Central America may be a test, but not of the type Mr. Kissinger suggests. It is rather a challenge to American political imagination, faith in traditional values, and the public's understanding of what constitutes strength and security in a nuclear age.

Notes

1. Speech by Ronald Reagan to a Joint Session of the Congress, Washington, D.C., April 27, 1983.
2. Three heads of U.S. missions in Central America and the Caribbean: Robert White (El Salvador), Lawrence Pezzullo (Nicaragua) and Wayne Smith (Cuba) were replaced by men with less experience and knowledge of the region after Reagan became president. In May 1983, Reagan removed Thomas Enders from his post as Assistant Secretary of State for Inter-American Affairs, reportedly because he suggested negotiations with the Salvadoran left. See *Washington Post*, May 28, 1983.

In 1983, Reagan removed Robert White's successor, Deane Hinton, and Francis MacNeil (Costa Rica), reportedly because they too had failed to pursue a hard enough line. In January 1984, it was announced that Anthony Quainton (Nicaragua) and Frederick Chapin (Guatemala) would be replaced. Quainton allegedly offended Henry Kissinger, chairman of the National Bipartisan Commission on Central America, by praising Nicaragua's progress in education and health care. Chapin was said to oppose the Pentagon's involvement in the revival of CONDECA. See *Washington Post*, January 5, 1984.

3. Eldon Kenworthy estimated Nicaragua's non-military trade with the Soviet Union and Eastern Europe at 6 percent of its total trade in 1982. See Eldon Kenworthy, "Central America: Beyond the Credibility Gap," *World Policy Journal*, Fall 1983, p. 189. For military procurements, Nicaragua turned to the Soviet Union, Eastern Europe and non-aligned nationalist regimes such as Algeria and Libya only after they were turned down by Western European nations and the United States. France did make a $15.8 million arms deal with Nicaragua in January 1982, but under pressure from the United States it did not renew military assistance. See *Los Angeles Times*, January 8, 1982; *Washington Post*, January 9, 1982. According to Rafael Solis, the Sandinista government's first ambassador to the United States, the Pentagon refused in late 1979 and early 1980 to consider selling military equipment to Nicaragua until an arms debt incurred by the Somoza regime had been paid. The Nicaraguans regarded this rebuff as politically motivated. Interview with Rafael Solis, January 14, 1984, by Peter Kornbluh.

4. Reagan, *op. cit.*

5. *New York Times*, July 19, 1983.

1

Origins of the Crisis

Not understood by the American public, and concealed by the Reagan Administration, is that the Latin American military—Salvadoran, Guatemalan or Argentine—routinely employs terror to exterminate guerrillas and insurgency movements. Devised by the Nazis for occupied Europe, perfected by Argentina and now passed from hand to hand by Latin military staffs, the strategy involves torture and murder of anyone suspected of association with "subversives." Guilt or innocence is immaterial; the object is to exterminate the opposition and, by cowing sympathizers into submission, deprive the guerrillas of support.

For the United States, which led the crusade against Nazi evil, to support the methods of Heinrich Himmler's extermination squads is an outrage.

Charles Maechling, Jr.
Head of State Dept. Counterinsurgency
and Internal Defense Planning
1961-1966

Introduction

In Guatemala, Honduras, El Salvador and Nicaragua, a few dozen families have controlled the lion's share of the national wealth since the Spanish conquest. In the late 19th century, the region's major landlords began to move into large-scale export agriculture, which required that they consolidate their holdings into plantation size units, viable for large-scale coffee growing and other export crops. Together with U.S.-based fruit companies, which took over large plots of land in Guatemala and

Honduras, the landed elite came to control most of Central America's best agricultural land. In this process, they dispossessed thousands of peasant and Indian families from communal lands, converting them into landless seasonal laborers.

During the mid-20th century, the landowners gradually mechanized production and introduced new export crops like cotton, which stimulated the elite to expand their near-monopoly control of the land. By the early 1960s, 3.7 percent of Guatemala's farms accounted for 68 percent of the country's agricultural land. In Honduras, 2.4 percent of the farms took up 48 percent of the land. In Nicaragua, 11 percent of the country's farms occupied 73 percent of the land. In 1971, 7.3 percent of El Salvador's farms took up 83 percent of the country's agricultural land.[1]

The peasantry was left to grow subsistence crops on marginal plots or to earn meager wages as a rural proletariat working on the plantations. By 1978, as a result of a century of this kind of impoverishment, approximately 75 percent of Salvadoran, Guatemalan and Honduran children under the age of five were malnourished, a phenomenon that has worsened over the last half decade.[2]

For the last hundred years in these four countries,[3] reformers and revolutionaries have periodically sought to overturn social systems that granted a small ruling elite economic and political control and condemned the majority to poverty, hunger and exploitation. The ruling elites have clung tenaciously to their wealth and privileges. The pages of Central American history run red with the blood of hundreds of thousands killed and tortured in order to stave off social change.

In general, the United States has stood with the ruling elites. The oligarchies have learned to shout "communism" at the merest whisper of reform, thereby linking their own survival to U.S. national security.[4] Ignoring the social roots of the conflicts now raging in Central America, the Reagan administration has revived a long tradition of U.S. intervention, using the CIA against Nicaragua, supplying and training the armed forces of El Salvador, and turning Honduras into a U.S. base.

The Nicaraguan and Salvadoran revolutions developed from 50 years of intense struggle in their own countries, and acquired an anti-American temper both from the experience of repeated U.S. intervention and from witnessing U.S. behavior—which repeatedly ignored the plight of the poor in favor of maintaining the status quo.

Throughout the first three decades of the century, U.S. presidents sent troops on 28 separate occasions into Central America and the Caribbean. U.S. troops intervened in Nicaragua in 1894, 1896, 1898 and twice in 1899. The official reasons cited by the State Department for the troop landings were: "to protect American interests...during political unrest" and "to protect American interests...following a revolution." In 1903, marines landed both in Honduras, "during a period of revolutionary activity," and in Panama, where they remained for 11 years "to guard American interests." Four of the interventions were in Cuba, where the United States acted "to restore order...and establish a stable government after serious revolutionary activity" (1906-1909), "to protect American interests during an insurrection" (1917-1922), and in 1933 "during a revolution...." Invariably, U.S. intervention reinforced the status quo and U.S. troops fought against revolutionaries and reformers.

In Nicaragua, from 1912 until 1925, U.S. marines battled nationalist forces "to protect American interests during an attempted revolution," and from 1926-1933 "to protect the interests of the United States." This second occupation, according to the State Department, "included activity against the outlaw Sandino," who is today known as the father of the Nicaraguan revolution.[5]

From Overt to Covert Operations

The tradition of intervention during the first decades of the 20th century was at least implicitly renounced in the post-World War II period when the United States signed the United Nations (UN) and Organization of American States (OAS) charters, which specifically outlawed armed interventions. These legal limitations coincided with the post-World War II commitments to democracy and human rights. But the roots of cold war policy, with its emphasis on national security, were planted at the same time. The United States had emerged from the war as the world's principal financial and industrial center, and with sole possession of the atomic bomb. The overwhelming power of the United States allowed it to set the terms of international relations in the post-war world, and America took on responsibility for policing the globe against communism.

To manage these new responsibilities, Congress authorized the creation of a permanent set of peacetime national security institutions, including a global network of military forces and intelligence operatives.[6] National security became an official doctrine in its own right, with the creation of national security bureaucracies, which were carefully insulated from the public debate characteristic of domestic policy.[7]

The commitments to nonintervention contained in the UN and the OAS charters came to be viewed not as legal norms obligating the United States to certain standards of international behavior, but as utopian ideals—inappropriate guides to behavior in the harsh world of *Realpolitik*. Intervention by U.S. military forces and the CIA became a major instrument for the preservation of "national security." Covert operations also became linked to specific U.S. economic interests in Central America. The most dramatic example came in 1954, when the CIA sponsored a coup which overthrew the democratically elected reformist government of Jacobo Arbenz in Guatemala. Although the United Fruit Company, with major interests in Guatemala, played a strong role in lobbying for the U.S. action, the State Department officially invoked an alleged "communist menace" as the rationale for overthrowing Arbenz.[8]

While U.S. global policy in the 1950s was fixated on containing communism, important social changes were taking place throughout Central America and the Caribbean. By the mid-1950s, a growing sector of the Central American middle class had become disturbed by the extremes of inequality, and had developed a political will to match its education. Arguing that the fundamental principles of western law and society were being violated in their countries, members of this new class began to challenge the entrenched aristocracy in national and regional politics. Often to their own surprise, they found that their reformist stance brought them into conflict with the U.S. government as well.

The Cuban Revolution and the Alliance for Progress

The event that shook the hemisphere, however, was the triumph of the Cuban Revolution in January 1959, an event that brought the Soviet Union into the affairs of the Caribbean.

Three months after the triumph of the Cuban revolution, U.S. disapproval began to take the form of punitive policies, which in turn helped induce a radicalization of the Cuban revolution. Cuba initiated a socialist path of development and in early 1960 called upon the Soviet Union for aid. By then, the U.S. government had begun planning an invasion of Cuba which turned into the April 1961 "Bay of Pigs" fiasco.[9]

A rapidly escalating U.S. campaign of economic sanctions was also initiated against Cuba, beginning in mid-1959. Credit was cut, trade curtailed and Cuba's sugar quota cancelled; by early 1961, a full-scale economic embargo was in place.[10]

While trying to overthrow the Cuban government on the one hand, President John F. Kennedy also sought to counter the Cuban revolution's influence in the rest of Latin America, most notably through the "Alliance for Progress." Kennedy recognized that "our unfulfilled task is to demonstrate to the entire world that man's unsatisfied aspiration for economic progress and social justice can best be achieved by free men working within a framework of democratic institutions." He acknowledged past U.S. errors, but promised that his new policy would rectify them:

> I have called on all people of the hemisphere to join in a new Alliance for Progress—*Alianza para Progresso*—a vast cooperative effort, unparalleled in magnitude and nobility of purpose, to satisfy the basic needs of the American people for homes, work and land, health and schools—*techo, trabajo y tierra, salud y escuela.*

"To complete the revolution of the Americas," he declared. . . "political freedom must accompany material progress. . . *progress si, tirania no!*"[11]

But the Kennedy program did not achieve its political objectives. The United States undertook to help finance infrastructure investments such as roads, harbors and telecommunications, while at the same time modernizing the region's military forces to prevent the tide of revolution from outpacing U.S.-sponsored reform. The basic U.S. objective in Latin America after the Cuban revolution was straightforward: to ensure that no other Cubas would emerge. Addressing the issue of U.S. policy toward Dominican dictator Rafael Trujillo, Kennedy stated that "there are three possibilities in descending order of preference: A decent democratic regime, a continuation of the despotic Trujillo regime or a Castro regime. We ought to aim at the first, but we can't really renounce the second until we are sure we can avoid the third."[12]

The emphasis on the military aspect of the policy produced growth without social or economic development. In 1963-64, the United States established the Central American Defense Council (CONDECA), a regional counterinsurgency force coordinated by the military heads of El Salvador, Honduras, Guatemala and Nicaragua. In Guatemala, U.S. special forces participated in a rural counterinsurgency campaign and advised security forces on how to counter urban radicalism.[13] In this process, an estimated 6,000-8,000 Guatemalan peasants were killed, and death squads in the cities eliminated political opponents whose views ranged from far left to right-of-center.[14] In El Salvador, a monopoly of political power remained in the hands of the military and the ruling families. Like the National Guard in Nicaragua, the Salvadorans received new weapons and advanced counterinsurgency training from the United States. The edifice of progress seemed to crumble as quickly as it was erected. Amid worsening economic conditions in 1969, war broke out between El Salvador and Honduras, turning CONDECA into little more than a paper structure. The five-day "soccer war," and the coincident economic decline throughout the region,[15] demonstrated the limits of the Central American Common Market in a region where the oligarchies would not cooperate in the interests of shared economic and political goals.

By the time the world economy was shaken by the OPEC-related price rises for oil and industrial imports in the mid-1970s, the Alliance for Progress had already faded as had hopes for reform through electorcal politics or constitutional means. Christian Democrats and Social Democrats alike, who had tried to tie themselves to Kennedy's Alliance language and create some political space for reforms, fell victim to the newly modernized military establishments which the United States had created in parallel to its Alliance growth strategy.

When, in 1972, Christian Democratic presidential candidate José Napoleon Duarte and his Social Democratic vice-presidential running mate Guillermo Ungo won El Salvador's first universally recognized fair election in 42 years, the military stepped in and nullified the results by force. In 1976, Nicaraguan liberals and conservatives pleaded in vain with General Anastasio Somoza to allow a political opening. In Guatemala, each tiny step toward reform was countered by political assassinations or right-wing military coups. During the Nixon and Ford administrations, the United States ignored these struggles for moderate or centrist reform.

The absence of genuine avenues for political expression combined with the inspiration provided by the Cuban revolution, encouraged some intellectuals and professionals to seek nationalist solutions, often linking their politics with Latin American revolutionary heroes of the past. In the 1970s, the Sandinista National Liberation Front (FSLN, formed in 1962 and named after the guerrilla leader who fought the Marines), and followers of the legendary peasant organizer Farabundo Marti, began to wage guerrilla war in Nicaragua and El Salvador. In Guatemala, a number of organizations, some closely tied to the Indians who make up a majority of the country's population, took up arms as their predecessors had in the 1960s.[16]

Running parallel to development of guerrilla activity in the 1970s were a number of efforts at legal, popular organizing, including elements borrowed from the Peace Corps, cooperative ventures and Christian and Social Democratic attempts to organize labor unions and peasant leagues.

From the late 1960s, the Catholic church had also begun to change. Allied for centuries with the oligarchy and the military, parts of the Church began to identify structural and systemic causes for poverty and to call for change.[17]

On the eve of the Carter administration, Marxist-oriented guerrilla forces, liberation theologians, and social democratic organizers who had managed to survive the repression began to come together in informal coalitions around their common acceptance of an inescapable reality: Peaceful avenues for reform were non-existent. They awaited the response of the new U.S. administration which had promised a new foreign policy, grounded less on the use of military force and more on a commitment to human rights and self-determination.

The Carter Years

The Carter administration set new guidelines for foreign policy, which appeared to challenge the dominance of the national security considerations that had shaped U.S. foreign policy since World War II. As a standard for judging U.S. behavior abroad, human rights coincided with deep-seated American traditions, and with liberal thinking as it had evolved since the end of the Vietnam war. But in order to reshape policy, human rights advocates would have had to present a formidable challenge to covert operations and counterinsurgency warfare, a task they lacked the power to accomplish. Instead, the Carter administration became locked in ambiguity, unable to resolve the conflicts between human rights concerns and fears of revolution.[18]

In Central America, these contradictory goals produced a policy that seemed always to be running to catch up with events. President Carter never made a clear choice in Nicaragua; there, as in El Salvador, he tried to promote a centrist compromise, a government that would respect human rights and undertake reforms while remaining within the U.S. sphere of influence.

The Nicaraguan insurrection in 1978 and 1979 posed several challenges. On the one hand, human rights guidelines should have precluded support for the brutal Somoza regime, but on the other, the national security bureaucracy's fear of another Cuba stalled the human rights advocates. The Administration advocated, but failed to secure, an OAS intervention in June 1979. It then tried to manipulate Nicaraguan politics in order to forge a pro-U.S. centrist government.[19] That plan also failed because all segments of Nicaraguan society contacted by the United States had already thrown their support behind the Sandinista junta and refused to backtrack.

But Carter still hoped to foster a moderate center in post-revolutionary Nicaragua. Administration planners targeted some $75 million in U.S. economic aid to the Nicaraguan private and public sectors, which they hoped would strengthen the country's most influential businessmen.[20] As the Sandinistas sought to rally world opinion and resources to reconstruct their war-ravaged nation, the Carter administration made clear that conditions would be attached to its aid, and the Sandinistas were strongly advised to limit Cuban influence.

Carter policy did not take seriously enough the nationalist origins of the Nicaraguan revolution, which drew primary inspiration from Augusto César Sandino, who had fought occupying U.S. Marines some 50 years earlier. The modern Sandinistas viewed with suspicion a U.S. president who had tried to keep them from power and warned them against Cuban influence.

The Sandinista victory in Nicaragua in 1979 had a powerful effect on events in nearby El Salvador.[21] Alarmed by the collapse of Somoza's National Guard and encouraged by the Carter administration, a group of reform-minded officers staged a coup against the corrupt and brutal regime of General Carlos Humberto Romero in October of 1979. A new junta and cabinet were formed, including a number of progressive civilians.[22]

But by the end of 1979, the unreformed military officials had regained control. The civilians in the government were unable to enact significant reforms or stop the security forces' repression against political organizers and demonstrators.

In January 1980 the civilian junta and cabinet members resigned *en masse* in protest. A facade of civilian participation was preserved when leaders of the Christian Democratic Party agreed to join in a new junta with the army. But the murder of Christian Democrat Attorney General Mario Zamora by a "death squad" in February, and the killings of hundreds of peasant and labor activists (a total of 527 were assassinated from January to March) persuaded the progressive wing of the Christian Democrats to leave the government.[23] They left the Christian Democratic Party as well, forming the Popular Social Christian Movement.[24]

The political opening of October 1979 had slammed shut. Middle class Social and Christian Democrats, seeing their political options curtailed, moved into opposition and allied themselves with the leftist guerrillas. In April, the Democratic Revolutionary Front (FDR) was formed, incorporating the Popular Social Christian Movement, social democratic and left parties, mass organizations, trade union federations and professional associations.

The Carter administration had proved no more successful at building a center in El Salvador than it had in Nicaragua. The internal contradictions of its foreign policy had prevented it from acting decisively against the right-wing erosion of the gains made by the October 1979 junta, because the national security bureaucracy pointed to the increasing strength of the left in El Salvador as the critical factor, and used this as an argument for maintaining U.S. support for the military.

In the final days of his administration, Carter approved a $5 million emergency injection of military aid into El Salvador, crossing the threshhold of "lethal" aid, to help the government hold off a guerrilla "final offensive." The dilemma posed by human rights and anti-communism as guidelines had been resolved. The human rights activists lost.

In 1980, 9,000–10,000 Salvadoran civilians were killed.[25] The Catholic Church attributed the vast majority of these deaths to the Salvadoran security forces and right-wing death squads. When Carter left office, the Salvadoran government was opposed not only by armed guerrillas, but by a broad popular coalition, led by one of the members of the October junta.[26] Moreover, Carter had provided the incoming Republican administration with the policy foundations to pursue a military solution in El Salvador and covert action against Nicaragua.

The Reagan Policy

Reagan began his campaign for the presidency by placing the Soviet Union and Cuba at the center of the debate over Central America. When Soviet troops marched into Afghanistan in December 1979, candidate Reagan called for a U.S. naval blockade of Cuba. In March 1980, speaking before the Chicago Council of Foreign Relations, he declared that "the Caribbean is being made, by way of Cuba, the Soviets' surrogate, into a red lake."[27] Speech by speech, statement by statement, Reagan committed himself to this narrow simplistic diagnosis of world events.

From the Santa Fe Committee to the Heritage Foundation, groups of right-wing intellectuals put forth strategies for the Caribbean and Central America, all of which presumed that events in the region were a vital test for U.S. national security.[28] By the time the Republican platform was issued in July 1980, the Party itself announced in thinly disguised language that it would support counterrevolutionary efforts against Nicaragua and abandon the Carter human rights policies:

> We deplore the Marxist Sandinista takeover of Nicaragua and Marxist attempt to destabilize El Salvador, Guatemala and Honduras...We will support the efforts of the Nicaraguan people to establish a free and independent government...We will return to the fundamental principle of treating a friend as a friend, and self-proclaimed enemies as enemies, without apology.

Central America, declared U.N. Ambassador Jeane Kirkpatrick, "is the most important place in the world."[29] Secretary of State Alexander Haig warned that it was the place where the United States "would draw the line."[30]

Where the Carter administration had vacillated, the Reagan administration made a clear choice: Human rights would run a poor second to anti-communism. El Salvador offered the Reagan administration a chance to demonstrate its new toughness. Administration officials also thought it would be an easy victory.

The Reagan administration rapidly turned its support for the Salvadoran government into a public crusade. The first public relations ploy was the "White Paper" released in February 1981, titled "Communist Interference in El Salvador."[31] This collection of documents was said by the Administration to prove that the Soviet Union, working through various surrogates, was directly financing and arming the Salvadoran guerrillas. In Europe and Latin America, Reagan launched a diplomatic campaign to convince the allies both that the charges of Soviet interference were genuine and that the anti-Soviet struggle in the region was essential to U.S. national security. The paper won initial credibility from the press and Congress, until several investigative reporters began to scrutinize the documents.

On June 8, 1981, the *Wall Street Journal* published a devastating critique of the White Paper, casting doubt on its evidence, methods and conclusions. Most damaging of all, it cited the State Department official who did most of the work on the document, Jon Glassman, as the source for its refutation.[32] The *Journal's* critique showed that the White Paper's conclusions about Soviet arms deliveries to El Salvador were not based on documentary evidence, but that Glassman's figures were "extrapolated." Although the White Paper was discredited, and the Administration has yet to produce evidence to prove the charge of significant Soviet, Cuban or Nicaraguan gun-running to El Salvador, the Administration has continued to repeat its assertions.

In 1982, U.S. Ambassador to El Salvador Deanne Hinton told a closed Senate Foreign Relations Committee meeting in response to a query about how many arms had actually been seized after Congress had appropriated $19 million to the CIA for that purpose: "Not a pistola, Senator."[33]

Unable to prove its case against the guerrillas, now federated in the Faribundo Marti National Liberation Front (FMLN), the Reagan administration has attempted to bolster the image of the Salvadoran government, and resisted pressures for negotiations with the left. The United States helped the Salvadoran government prepare for the Constituent Assembly elections of March 1982, which were intended to present the image of a pluralist democracy at work, and simultaneously demonstrate that the guerrillas were politically marginal. The left opposition excluded itself from the electoral process on the grounds that its members risked death by campaigning publicly. When the FDR leaders had come into San Salvador in November 1980 to meet with members of the government they were assassinated by security forces.[34] An election was held and when the votes were counted, El Salvador had a rightist Constituent Assembly headed by former Major Roberto D'Aubuisson, a man described as a "pathological killer" by former U.S. Ambassador Robert White.[35] (White has implicated D'Aubuisson in the murders of Archbishop Oscar Romero and Attorney General Mario Zamora in early 1980.) Since its inception, the Assembly has reversed, frozen or undermined most reform programs, including the much-heralded agrarian reform.[36]

The Reagan administration has opposed negotiations for ending the war and sharing power between the Salvadoran government and the FDR-FMLN, insisting that the left must first put down its arms and participate in elections. In other words, Reagan administration policy remains wedded to military victory over the left.[37]

But the Salvadoran army has not proved effective, despite U.S. backing, training and advice. More accustomed to repressing civilians than fighting armed and organized combatants, and notorious for its corruption, the Salvadoran army responded to the insurgency with battalion-size daylight sweeps through rural areas. This tactic failed to eliminate the highly mobile rebels, although it did result in the destruction of villages and the massacre of civilians. U.S. advisors pressed for the adoption of more sophisticated counterinsurgency tactics, urging continuous patrolling by the small units in order to "take the night away from the guerrillas" and occupy areas rather than just move through them. In the summer of 1983, the United States got its way. A counterinsurgency campaign, known as the National Plan, was launched in the central provinces of San Vicente and Usalatán. But as the army began using smaller units—360-man "hunter" battalions broken down into 90-man companies—and concentrating its forces in the two selected provinces, the guerrillas melted away. Then in the fall, they countered the National Plan by launching large-scale attacks in other provinces. By 1984, the U.S.-inspired National Plan was in disarray, with the guerrillas returning and occupying substantial portions even of San Vicente and Usalatán. Despite hundreds of millions of dollars in U.S. aid and extensive U.S. training, the Salvadoran army had ended 1983 in its worst position since the beginning of the war.

The Reagan administration has taken out much of its frustration on Nicaragua. Following the rhetoric of the Republican Party's 1980 platform, and seeking to regain what the Carter administration "lost," ever-increasing efforts have been made to overthrow the Sandinistas.

Although Administration officials have called Nicaragua's government "totalitarian" and a "Soviet surrogate," the Nicaraguan revolution does not fit that mold. The leading factions in the Sandinista coalition were formed over the objections of the small, Moscow-oriented communist party in Nicaragua.[38] The pluralist economy (with a private sector which in 1981 produced about 60 percent of the gross national product) bears no resemblance to Soviet or Cuban models of centralized planning.[39] The Sandinistas have begun to create a new class of landowning small farmers, moving in exactly the opposite direction from Soviet collectivization of agriculture. The latitude accorded the Catholic Church and the religious elements of the revolution itself are dramatically different from Soviet attitudes and practices toward organized religion.

Moreover, Nicaragua explicitly has sought to avoid becoming dependent upon the U.S.S.R. Through 1981, 49 percent of its external bilateral aid came from the West; less than 20 percent came from Cuba and the Soviet Union.[40] Nicaragua did receive, according to the State Department, "between $175 and $200 million in military assistance from the Soviet Union," mostly in 1982-83, and "tens of millions" of dollars from

Cuba and East European nations. Nicaragua's attempts to procure arms from the West, including the United States, have proven difficult. France sold Nicaragua $11 million in military goods in 1982, but is not likely to renew its sales offer because of pressure from the Reagan administration. The bulk of Nicaragua's non-military trade remains with the West or the Third World; less than 20 percent is with the COMECON countries.

Nevertheless, Nicaragua has been targeted for destabilization. In 1980, Argentina agreed to send military advisors to Honduras to train a force established in that country to harass Nicaragua. The intelligence services of Venezuela and Colombia, and later Israel, promised that their officials would work with the CIA in an overall plan to overthrow the Sandinista government. Meanwhile in Washington, CIA Director William Casey told Congress that the operation was minimal and that U.S. allies were doing the dirty work, so that Congress need not fear that previous illegal and unpopular CIA operations would be repeated. The goal, Casey assured nervous members, was to "attack the Cuban infrastructure" in Nicaragua; later this was changed to "interdicting" Nicaraguan arms supplies to El Salvador.[41] The State Department charged that there were some 2,000 Cuban military advisors in Nicaragua, a figure dismissed as exaggerated by Nicaraguan officials. In fact, the Cubans had hundreds of teachers, doctors, and non-military advisors in the country. There were no Cuban physical installations in Nicaragua that could be attacked, and as U.S. officials later ascertained, there was no significant arms supply to interdict.[42]

By November 1981, CIA chief Casey was seriously understating the Administration's covert action goals against Nicaragua, telling the congressional oversight committees that the $19 million budget being requested for the project was simply for "interdiction" of arms. In fact, the Administration was building up an infrastructure in Honduras with which to wage war against the Sandinistas from two land fronts, and planning a series of naval maneuvers combined with land and air operations which, upon presidential command, could be transformed into a full-scale invasion. A defecting Argentine intelligence agent later charged, in an account confirmed by congressional sources, that the CIA had used other governments, mainly Argentina, to carry out the tasks that Casey had told Congress the CIA was not undertaking. He disclosed that the covert war against Nicaragua involved a network of vast proportions, which included the financing of foreign officials as well as officers and foot soldiers in the counterrevolutionary army. The CIA also began to recruit former Green Berets to carry out secret missions inside Nicaragua. Campaigns to sabotage Nicaraguan installations were plotted in Costa Rica and Honduras.[43]

The CIA tried to explain to puzzled members of Congress that tying down the Sandinistas and harassing their militia made it more difficult for them to send arms to El Salvador, and that therefore the violence employed against Nicaraguan installations and personnel did fall under the definition of "interdiction."

The destabilization campaign[44] drew growing—though private—concern in Congress and provoked leaders of Ecuador, Brazil, Venezuela, Mexico, Argentina and Peru to declare opposition to possible U.S. military intervention in Nicaragua.[45]

The U.S. destabilization policy also had an effect on events inside Nicaragua. The struggle for power and resources among the different sectors became polarized. The government declared a state of emergency on March 14, 1982, following the demolition of two bridges by U.S.-trained Nicaraguan saboteurs in northern Nicaragua.[46] Faced with war on two borders and a U.S. economic squeeze, the Sandinistas began to set more stringent limits for dissent and to mobilize militarily and politically. The internal political battle over the sharing of power was converted into a fight for national survival against an outside attacker backed by the United States.

The campaign against the Sandinistas has now begun to transform the region as a whole. The Reagan administration has tried to enlist peaceful Costa Rica in the anti-Sandinista cause, pressuring its government to augment its security forces and permit U.S. combat engineers to build roads and airstrips close to the Nicaraguan border. Honduras has been designated as the principal U.S. base in the region. It is providing encampments for the Nicaraguan counterrevolutionaries *(contras)* and has cooperated with the Salvadoran army in the massacre of Salvadoran refugees, most notably at the Rio Sumpul on May 14, 1980, and the Rio Lempa on March 18, 1981. A large U.S. training base has been constructed at Puerto Castilla, on the Honduran Atlantic coast, in order to train Salvadoran troops. The United States has built a half-dozen new military airfields in Honduras, all suitable for the largest military transport aircraft. Two powerful radar stations have been set up in Honduras, with a range that covers most of the Central American region.

A series of military exercises has been held in Honduras, the most recent of which is "Big Pine II," a six-month series of joint maneuvers and training exercises involving as many as 6,000 U.S. troops at one time. A U.S. command center has been established in central Honduras with some 1,500 U.S. military personnel.

Direct aid to the Honduran military has quadrupled since 1981, and the power of General Gustavo Álvarez Martínez, head of the Honduran Armed Forces, overshadows that of the civilian government. Honduran security forces, answerable only to Álvarez, have begun perpetrating "disappearances" and political murders in a country where such practices were almost unknown a few years ago. Between 1981 and October 1983, 62 Hondurans "disappeared" and 47 political assassinations were carried out.[47]

Alvarez has helped the United States revive the Central American Defense Council (CONDECA), which now includes Panama as an observer.[48]

1984: A Failure of Policy on All Fronts

In January 1984, President Reagan can point to few successes in the region. The Administration has increased the U.S. commitment to anti-revolutionary forces, and its military and CIA policies offer little hope for improvement.

The CIA's undeclared war against Nicaragua has intensified as its budget requests have gone well beyond the initial $19 million. But its forces have been unable to score battlefield victories or secure significant territory. To be sure, they have inflicted severe damage on port facilities and destroyed oil pipelines and refineries; they also continue to kill Nicaraguan civilians. The U.S. economic campaign has succeeded in cutting off most private bank funds and multilateral financing to Nicaragua. But in defiance of Reagan administration policy, several European allies of the United States maintain aid programs, and in 1983, Sweden doubled its assistance to the Sandinista government. Mexico continues to supply subsidized oil to Nicaragua.[49] In January 1984, another blow was dealt to the Reagan policy when Argentine President Raul Alfonsin announced that he was officially withdrawing Argentine support for covert actions against Nicaragua.

In El Salvador, the poor performance of the army and the guerrilla successes of late December and early January 1984, tend to dispel the notion that the Salvadoran military can win without direct intervention by U.S. troops.

Flagrant human rights abuses by the security forces remain an embarrassment to the Reagan administration. During late 1983, the death squads became particularly active in attempts to destroy the guerrillas' infrastructure—the thousands of sympathetic civilians who provide food, information, supplies, medical care and other assistance to the combatants. As with the Phoenix program in Vietnam, assassination teams have killed thousands of civilians suspected of sympathy for the left, including teachers, trade unionists and health workers. Also targeted have been political leaders thought to favor talks with FDR/FMLN representatives. The overall civilian death toll is 37,000 for the last four years, most of which is attributed to death squads or uniformed security forces.[50] So troublesome have the killings become to Reagan policy that Vice President George Bush travelled to El Salvador in December of 1983 to warn Salvadoran officials that death squad activity would jeopardize U.S. support.[51]

The one "victory" that President Reagan can claim in the region is the successful October 1983 U.S. invasion of Grenada, sweeping away a revolutionary government which had already been all but liquidated by its own militants. This precipitous invasion, along with the Administration's repeated rebuffs of Nicaraguan peace proposals, diminished the Reagan administration's international prestige. European and Latin American leaders were openly critical of the invasion of Grenada, and some expressed fears that this would embolden the Administration to undertake further military adventures, particularly in Central America.

The historical role played by the United States in Latin America has undercut the ability of the Reagan administration to win support for its policies from Latin Americans. The repeated military interventions throughout the 20th century in Latin America were carried out not by Soviet forces, but by the United States. The specter of the Soviet bogeyman is not a strong selling point for most educated Latin Americans. The historical enemies of freedom and justice in the small countries of Central America have not been communists, much less Soviets, but the ruling aristocracies whose militaries have been trained by the United States and by U.S. forces themselves.

President Reagan has failed to address the deeply-held nationalist feelings and ideas of the region and has ignored the social and economic system that has produced the massive unrest. By imposing the ill-fitting East–West framework on Central America, he has squeezed himself into a corner. Since U.S. commitment to defeat revolution has been equated with fighting the Soviets, the very notion of the left winning is viewed as the equivalent to a major Soviet victory. Thus the nation faces a tragic choice of its own making—a self-proclaimed defeat of major proportions or a direct U.S. military intervention in El Salvador or Nicaragua.

Notes

1. James W. Wilkie and Stephen Haber, eds., *Statistical Abstract of Latin America*, Volume 21 (Los Angeles: UCLA Latin American Center Publications, University of California, 1981), p. 58.
2. Inter-American Development Bank, *Economic and Social Progress in Latin America: 1978 Report*. Washington, D.C.: IDB, 1978, p. 138.
3. The general patterns of Central America do not apply to Costa Rica for several reasons. At the time of the Spanish conquest, the area then named Costa Rica did not have a large indigenous population. Since there were only a few Indians to enslave, the feudal system of the "Hacienda" was not developed as it was in Guatemala, Honduras, El Salvador and Nicaragua. When independence came, Costa Rica still was the least populated of the five Central American provinces and the most primitive. After the war against the U.S. "filibusters" under William Walker was won, Costa Rica embarked on a development process that was different from the other republics. Since the 1850s, Costa Rica promoted and succeeded in attracting a relatively large inflow of European immigrants, mainly from northern Spain, who settled in the country's "meseta central" and developed not only modern farming but also a democratic form of government.

   A more racially homogeneous population and a more equitable distribution of the coffee proceeds in the late 19th century allowed even poor peasants to feel that they had a stake in their society. Further, Costa Ricans had learned that a military does little to protect small countries from outside enemies, and that the armed forces of Central American countries frequently become the enemy of the majority. Costa Ricans opted not to build an institutionalized military. See Carlos Monge Alfaro, Historia de Costa Rica (San Jose: 1960); Dwight Heath, "Costa Rica and Her Neighbors." Current History 58, February, 1970.
4. Former Salvadoran president Jose Napoleon Duarte describes the phenomenon in his country: "Communists have been the scapegoat for everything here...People had to avoid even thinking about change to avoid being called a Communist, even though the Communist Party was very small." See *Los Angeles Times*, December 18, 1983.
5. All quotations in this paragraph and the one that precedes it are taken from Dean Rusk, "Instances of the Use of United States Armed Forces Abroad, 1798-1945," Hearing before the Committee on Foreign Relations and the Committee on Armed Services, 87th Congress, 2nd Session, September 17, 1962.
6. The National Security Act of 1947 authorized the creation of the National Security Council (NSC) and the Central Intelligence Agency (CIA), and unified the armed forces into the Department of Defense. The National Security Agency (NSA) was established in 1952. See Morton H. Halperin, Jerry L. Berman, Robert L. Borosage,

and Christine M. Marwick, *The Lawless State* (New York: Penguin, 1976), pp. 15, 172. President Lyndon Johnson called U.S. forces "guardians at the gate," defending the free world from communism. Quoted in Richard Pfeffer, ed., *No More Vietnams? The War and the Future of American Foreign Policy* (New York: Harper and Row, 1968), p. 261.

7. Halperin et al., *op. cit.*, pp. 220-236. See also Robert L. Borosage, "The Making of the National Security State," in Leonard Rodberg and Derek Shearer, eds., *The Pentagon Watchers* (Garden City: Doubleday, 1982) pp. 90-97; Marcus G. Raskin, "Democracy Versus the National Security State," *Law and Contemporary Problems.* Vol. 40, No. 3, 1976, pp. 189-220.

8. Stephen Kinzer and Stephen Schlesinger, *Bitter Fruit* (Garden City: Doubleday, 1982), pp. 9-97.

9. See Peter Wyden, *Bay of Pigs: The Untold Story* (New York: Simon and Schuster, 1979).

10. See Herbert Matthews, *Revolution in Cuba: An Essay in Understanding* (New York: Charles Scribner's Sons, 1975).

11. Arthur M. Schlesinger, *A Thousand Days* (Boston: Houghton-Mifflin, 1965), pp. 204-205.

12. *Ibid.*, p. 769.

13. Delia Miller, Roland Seeman, Cynthia Arnson, *Background on Guatemala, the Armed Forces and U.S. Military Assistance*, Washington, D.C.: Institute for Policy Studies Resource Report, June 1981, pp. 5-6.

14. Walter LaFeber, *Inevitable Revolutions* (New York: W.W. Norton, 1983), p. 170.

15. Annual economic growth for the countries of El Salvador, Guatemala, Honduras and Nicaragua averaged 5.9 percent during the 1960s. This average declined to 4.7 percent in the first half of the 1970s and to 3.7 percent in the second half of the decade. In 1981, only post-revolutionary Nicaragua showed positive growth while El Salvador had negative growth of 9.5 percent and Guatemala and Honduras were almost stagnant. See Inter-American Development Bank, *Economic and Social Progress in Latin America: 1980-1981 Report*, Washington, D.C.

16. In Nicaragua, the opposition traced its roots to the nationalist guerrilla leader, Augusto César Sandino, who fought an occupying force of U.S. Marines from 1927 to 1933. Before the Marines left, they set up the National Guard, and arranged for Anastasio Somoza to lead it. The Guard became a kind of praetorian army, loyal to the Somoza clan, and linked for training and weapons for most of its institutional life to the U.S. armed forces. During the 1970s, widespread opposition to Anastasio Somoza, the heir of the Somoza dynasty, emerged. By the mid-1970s, even sectors of the economic elite had become unhappy with the Somoza family's rapaciousness. Before their overthrow, the Somozas were Nicaragua's largest landowner and controlled about a quarter of the nation's industry. Using state resources, Anastasio Somoza amassed for himself and his family a fortune estimated at around $900 million. See *New York Times*, July 20, 1979.

The Sandinista Front for National Liberation (FSLN) was formed in 1962 as a clandestine revolutionary political and military movement, composed of peasants, urban workers, students and intellectuals. Within the Sandinistas, three "tendencies" emerged in the 1970s: one called for a war based in the countryside, a second stressed urban struggle, and the third, which prevailed, advocated "the unity of all opposition forces, whatever their class character, around a broad program of social reform and democracy." This latter "tendency" successfully forged alliances with middle-class groups. In 1979, after 15 years of activity, the Sandinistas were recognized as the leading opposition force to Somoza. See William LeoGrande, "The Revolution in Nicaragua: Another Cuba?" *Foreign Affairs*, Vol. 58, No. 1, Fall 1979, p. 32. For information on the Church's important role in the Nicaraguan revolution, see *NACLA Report on the Americas*, Vol. XV, No. 3, May-June 1981, pp. 45-48.

In El Salvador, the military had taken power in 1931 from a weak civilian president. In the face of deep peasant unrest, the army demonstrated its intransigence the following year: General Maximiliano Hernandez Martinez, the self-proclaimed President, ordered the systematic slaughter of 10,000 to 30,000 peasants after an abortive uprising. A committed theosophist, Hernandez Martinez believed in reincarnation. Hence, he said, "it is a greater crime to kill an ant than a man, because the man is born again at death, while the ant dies forever." See Cynthia Arnson, *El Salvador: A Revolution Confronts the United States*, (Washington, D.C.: IPS, 1982), p. 14. One of the current death squads is named after Hernandez Martinez.

By the 1970s, serious middle-class opposition to army rule had emerged and the Catholic Church became a major political actor, as priests sought to implement church doctrine developed during Vatican II and Medellin (see footnote 17). Between 1970 and 1976, priests trained 15,000 lay preachers and teachers on topics ranging from Bible study and liturgy to agriculture, cooperativism, leadership, and health, according to Tommie Sue Montgomery. The priests and lay leaders in turn established the so-called "Christian base communities," small groups of twenty or thirty people who met regularly for Bible study. From September 1973 to June 1974 alone, ten urban and twenty-seven rural base communities were organized. Participants in these groups learned, as Montgomery puts it, "that they are equal before God to the large hacienda owner down the road," and "that it is not God's will that people be poor." This message, Montgomery concludes, "was profoundly radicalizing in a political as well as a religious sense." See Tommie Sue Montgomery, *Revolution in El Salvador: Origins and Evolution*, (Boulder: Westview, 1982), pp. 102-107. Urban professionals and trade union federations joined with activists of the Christian Democratic Party and other opposition groups to protest the nullification by the military of the elections in 1972. In 1977, the military staged an election in the face of widespread outrage, but it was so fraudulent that not even the vote totals were announced. The military simply named its candidate, General Carlos Humberto Romero, the winner. One Salvadoran politician is said to have remarked: "In El Salvador not only do the votes not count, they are not even counted." See Manilio Tirado, *La Crisis Politica in El Salvador*, (Mexico: Ediciones Quinto Sol, 1980.)

In 1980, the Democratic Revolutionary Front (FDR) was formed. It included dissident Christian Democrats, Social Democrats, members of popular organizations, trade unions, professional organizations, student and religious groups. The FDR is the political counterpart of the Farabundo Marti National Liberation Front (FMLN), the military arm of the left-center alliance, which is composed of five guerrilla organizations.

The joint FDR-FMLN political platform calls for the replacement of the current regime with a broadly-based democratic government that would protect human rights and basic freedoms. Among the pledges are: comprehensive agrarian reform, health and literacy campaigns, nationalization of banking, and guarantees of protection for small- and medium-sized landholders and businessmen. In foreign policy, the FDR-FMLN pledges non-alignment. The FDR-FMLN has called for negotiations with the Salvadoran government and for the United States to end the war.

Since the CIA-backed coup overthrew the democratically-elected Arbenz government in 1954, Guatemala has had a series of harsh military dictatorships. Regular elections were held, but only right-wing parties were allowed to participate, and the winner was almost always a general. In 1979, two Social Democratic parties were allowed to register, but their leaders were promptly assassinated. Hundreds of political activists have been murdered by security forces, including leaders of peasant cooperatives, trade unionists and religious workers. In a 1981 publication entitled *Guatemala: A Government Program of Political Murder*, Amnesty International charged that nearly 5,000 Guatemalans had been murdered by the country's military regime since 1978. See Amnesty International, "Guatemala: A Government Program of

Political Murder," (London: Amnesty International, 1981), p. 5.

In February 1982, four Guatemalan guerrilla groups announced the formation of the Guatemalan National Revolutionary Unity (URNG), a joint political and military directorate. The URNG released a five-point program calling for an end "to repression against the people," "cultural oppression and discrimination," and "economic and political domination of the repressive local and foreign wealthy class," and promising to establish a representative government and adopt a non-aligned foreign policy. See *Foreign Broadcast Information Service*, February 10 and March 19, 1982. The statement made an appeal to both small- and medium-sized landowners, businessmen, and military officers not identified with official corruption and repression to join in the fight against the government.

Several days after the formation of the URNG, prominent Guatemalan exiles led by writer Luis Cardoza y Aragon announced the creation of the Guatemalan Patriotic Unity Committee (CGUP) to coordinate the international political work of the Guatemalan left. The CGUP, with over 50 leaders from opposition parties, unions, and professional organizations hopes to build unity among opposition sectors represented in the Democratic Front Against Repression (FDCR) and the Popular Front-31st of January (FP–31). The FDCR and FP–31 are coalitions of close to 200 peasant and labor unions, student, teacher, and professional groups, as well as opposition parties, including the Social Democrats.

17. This shift can be traced to the Second Vatican Council of the early 1960s, known as Vatican II, which sanctioned the Church's role in worldly matters, and affirmed the equality of its members. In 1968, Latin American bishops gathered in Medellin, Colombia, and decided that the Church must actively work with and for the poor and oppressed, a course reinforced at the next meeting of bishops in Puebla, Mexico in 1979. For an excellent discussion of the church in Latin America, see Penny Lernoux, *Cry of the People* (New York: Doubleday and Co., 1980).

18. "There are only two specific core values that policy makers are said to share and that thereby provide coherence for United States policy toward Latin America: anticommunism and support for the property rights of liberal capitalism, including free trade. It cannot be denied that the United States acts with extraordinary coherence when policy makers perceive a threat from a foreign enemy in Latin America and that since World War II the enemy has been labeled communism. Nor can it be denied that during the last three decades a variety of left-leaning Latin American political movements have been attacked by the U.S. government. Anti-communism is a real and prominent value informing United States policy toward Latin America.

"Because foreign policy officials view their primary responsibilities to be furthering the nation's interests abroad and protecting national security, humanitarian values never dominate foreign policy. After Latin America has been made safe from communism and for capitalism, however, a variety of humanitarian values tends to be expressed in U.S. foreign policy." See Lars Schoultz, *Human Rights and United States Policy Toward Latin America* (Princeton, New Jersey: Princeton University Press, 1981), pp. 366-367.

19. William LeoGrande, "The Revolution in Nicaragua: Another Cuba?" *Foreign Affairs*, Vol. 58, No. 1, Fall 1979, p. 36.

20. In October of 1980, the Carter administration obtained Congressional approval for a $70 million loan to Nicaragua, and a $5 million grant. The grant was targeted to U.S.-aligned organizations in Nicaragua. The loan was for the purchase of raw materials and machinery from the United States; 60 percent of it had to be made available to private businesses in Nicaragua. See Jeff McConnell, "America's Secret War," in Peter Rosset and John Vandermeer, eds., *The Nicaragua Reader*, (New York: Grove Press, 1983), p. 179.

21. Cynthia Arnson, *op. cit.*, pp. 34-36, and Walter LeFeber, *op. cit.* pp. 242-276. See also discussion in Tommie Sue Montgomery, *op. cit.*, pp. 55-76.

22. Included in the October junta were Guillermo Ungo, leader of the Social Democratic National Revolutionary Movement (MNR) and Ramon Mayorga, rector of the Jesuit Central American University. Members of the Christian Democratic Party, the Nationalist Democratic Union, and the MNR joined the junta's cabinet.

23. A group of six masked men who broke into Zamora's home during a meeting of leading Christian Democrats, singled out Zamora and shot him. A government official claimed two days later that then vice-minister of Defense Nicolas Carranza had been involved in the assassination. See Tommie Sue Montgomery, *op. cit.*, p. 167. Carranza is now director of the Treasury Police, the smallest but most notorious Salvadoran security force. Carranza's chief of intelligence was recently named by U.S. authorities as a death squad leader and has been transferred to an army post. See *Los Angeles Times*, December 18, 1983.

24. Hector Dada, a Christian Democrat who left the junta in March 1980, was replaced by Napoleon Duarte. Eight cabinet ministers and undersecretaries also resigned, including Finance Minister Roberto Alvergue Vides and Planning Minister Roberto Salazar Candell.

25. U.S. Department of State, *Country Reports on Human Rights Practices*, February 2, 1981, p. 429 (placing the figure at 9,000); Socorro Juridico, Arzobispado de San Salvador, 4 de Junio de 1981 (placing the number at 10,000). Quoted in Americas Watch and American Civil Liberties Union, *Report on Human Rights in El Salvador* (New York: Random House, 1982), p. 37.

26. Guillermo Ungo, leader of the Social Democratic Nationalist Revolutionary Movement (MNR), is president of the Democratic Revolutionary Front (FDR). Ungo had also been the vice-presidential candidate on the coalition ticket that won the 1972 presidential elections, only to have the results nullified by the military. Duarte was the presidential candidate.

27. Speech by Ronald Reagan, "Peace and Security in the 1980's," Chicago, Illinois, March 17, 1980.

28. Warning that the Caribbean "is becoming a Marxist-Leninist lake," a group of ultra-right intellectuals and a retired general calling themselves the Committee of Santa Fe issued a May 1980 publication, *A New Inter-American Policy for the Eighties*, which argues that "The United States is being shoved aside in the Caribbean and Central America by a sophisticated, but brutal, extracontinental superpower manipulating client states."

    The Heritage Foundation, founded in 1973 with seed money from Joseph Coors, is a Washington-based institute with close ties to the Reagan administration. It presented incoming President Reagan with a 1,200 page blueprint for policy in January 1981. Its major publication is *Mandate for Leadership: Policy Management in a Conservative Administration*, edited by Charles Heatherly and published in 1981.

    Senator Jesse Helms (R–N.C.), speaking to the National Conservative Political Action Conference in Washington, D.C. in April 1982, put into plain language the thinking of the far right on Central America:

    "Why are the media and many still in the State Department so eager to help the Marxist-Leninists come into power?...Why do they insist that Central American conservatives and anti-communists who want to be our friends and who are our friends should get out of the way and let these rebels, and whatever else they call 'em, take over. I say no. But it's obvious, the Soviet strategy is, and always has been, and always will be, to encircle and surround the United States with socialist nations." See *Quest for Power: Sketches of the New Right*, a film by Saul Landau and Frank Diamond, 1982.

29. *Newsweek*, March 16, 1981.

30. *Washington Post*, March 14, 1981.

31. U.S. Department of State, "Communist Interference in El Salvador." Special Report No. 80, Washington, D.C.: Department of State, February 23, 1981.

32. Glassman admitted to *Journal* reporter Jonathon Kwitny that parts of the White Paper might be "misleading" or "over-embellished" and that some "guessing" had gone into its conclusions. Moreover, the *Journal* article pointed out that a letter written by the head of the Salvadoran Communist Party, which was quoted in the White Paper as evidence of Soviet involvement, actually indicates a lack of Soviet interest in supplying arms to the Salvadoran left. See *Wall Street Journal*, June 8, 1981. Salvadoran rightist Roberto D'Aubuisson told *Albuquerque Journal* reporter Craig Pyes that he and his aides provided key material for the White Paper. It was solicited from him in 1980 by Reagan campaign adviser, retired Lt. Gen. Daniel O. Graham, who asked him to "furnish proof that would justify greater American intervention in Central America." See *Albuquerque Journal*, December 22, 1983.

33. Hinton's assessment was later backed up by numerous other sources. See footnote 42.

34. On November 27, 1980, Enrique Alvarez Cordova, a former Minister of Agriculture and president of the FDR, was kidnapped along with five other FDR leaders by a joint operation of security forces and civilian death squad members. Their mutilated bodies were found shortly thereafter.

35. Because D'Aubuisson was an embarrassment, the U.S. embassy and the Salvadoran high command successfully pressured the Constituent Assembly to appoint banker Alvaro Magaña as president.

36. The Salvadoran agrarian reform program was designed by University of Washington professor Roy Prosterman, who devised a similar program for South Vietnam in the late 1960s. For Prosterman's assessment of the land reform, see *The New Republic*, August 9, 1982. Also see Oxfam America, "El Salvador Land Reform: 1980-1981." Impact Audit. Boston: OXFAM America, 1982.

37. In his speech to the Baltimore Council on Foreign Affairs on September 12, 1983, Undersecretary of Defense Fred Ikle stated: "We do not seek a military defeat for our friends. We do not seek a military stalemate. We seek victory for the forces of democracy."

38. See discussion in Phil Berryman, "The Case for Accommodation: United States Policy Toward Central American Revolutions," A paper prepared for PACCA, October, 1983. Also, George Black, *Triumph of the People: The Sandinista Revolution in Nicaragua* (London: Zed Press, 1981), p. 72.

39. Tom Barry, Beth Wood and Deb Preusch, *Dollars and Dictators* (Albuquerque, N.M.: Resource Center, 1982), p. 218.

40. Junta of the Government of National Reconstruction, *The Philosophy and Policies of the Government of Nicaragua* (Managua: Direccion de Divulgacion y Prensa, March 1982), p. 13.

41. *New York Times*, December 17, 1982 and April 2, 1983; *Washington Post*, April 3, 1983 and May 8, 1983; *Miami Herald*, December 19, 1982; and *The Nation*, March 6, 1982. For background information on the covert war against Nicaragua, see *NACLA Report on the Americas*, Vol. XVI No. 1, Jan.-Feb. 1982.

42. Cuba and Nicaragua supplied a significant amount of arms to the Salvadoran guerrillas into early 1981. See Wayne Smith, "Myopic Diplomacy," *Foreign Policy*, No. 48, Fall, 1982, pp. 157-174. The arms flow later tapered off, according to reliable reports. By July 1983, a senior Reagan Administration official confirmed reports that Salvadoran guerrillas were receiving only small amounts of military assistance from Nicaragua. See *New York Times*, July 31, 1983. *Washington Post* reporter Christopher Dickey wrote that "for more than a year there has been very little solid evidence of material support for the Salvadorans originating in Nicaragua. See *Washington Post*, February 21, 1983. In March 1983, the *New York Times* reported that, "no significant weapons shipments have been intercepted on their way to El Salvador in the last two years." See *New York Times*, March 12, 1983. In subsequent months, according to United States military sources quoted by the *New York Times* in March 1983, most of the Salvadoran guerrillas' arms came from Salvadoran government supplies. See *New*

York Times, March 9, 1983. Reliable sources cited by Eldon Kenworthy estimate that 40 percent of the equipment the United States gives the Salvadoran army passes to the guerrillas. See Eldon Kenworthy, "Central America: Beyond the Credibility Trap," *World Policy Journal,* Fall 1983, p. 189.

43. Testimony of Hector Frances, translated by the Congressional Research Service, December 6, 1982. See also Saul Landau, "Prisoners of an Undeclared War," *Rolling Stone,* No. 393, April 14, 1983, pp. 11-12.

44. In late 1981, the Reagan administration suspended the undisbursed portion of the Carter administration's $75 million in aid to Nicaragua—$7 million. During the same period, U.S. funding to the *contras* began producing a series of sabotage actions.

45. Instituto Historico Centroamericano, *Envio.* Managua: December 1981.

46. *Washington Post,* May 8, 1983.

47. Committee for the Families of the Disappeared and Detained in Honduras (COFADEH), "Open Letter to the Conscience of the American People," Tegulcigalpa, November 30, 1983.

49. CONDECA had been weakened by the 1969 war between Honduras and El Salvador, and was finished off by the overthrow of Somoza. Recent efforts to reconstitute it as an anti-Nicaraguan bloc have hinged on Guatemala. The Rios Montt regime, which had resisted U.S. regional efforts and concentrated on fighting its own insurgency, was ousted by the more cooperative General Mejia Victores in August 1983. Echoing the Reagan administration view that Nicaragua represented the principal threat to the region, Mejia Victores agreed to participate in a new CONDECA. But more recently, Guatemala has become less cooperative as the United States Congress has refused to lift restrictions on military aid to that country.

49. Mexico supplies virtually all of Nicaragua's oil imports (which amount to $225 million per year) at a relatively inexpensive rate through a long-term credit arrangement.

50. The Salvadoran armed forces and right-wing death squads killed more than 37,000 Salvadorans between October 1979 and September 1983. Americas Watch, "Human Rights Update on Central America." Washington D.C.: Americas Watch, 1983, p. 3.

51. Alvaro Magana, the provisional president of El Salvador, announced that his country would be unable to fully comply with U.S. requests for the exiling of prominent civilian and military death squad figures. *Newsweek,* January 16, 1984, p. 25.

2

The Framework for Policy:
The National Interest

"The public. . . was hoodwinked by such methods as were used
and actually supposed our acquisition of the new territory to be
a God-fearing act, the result of the aggression and of the sinful
impotence of our Spanish neighbors, together with our own jus-
tifiable energy and our devotion to the cause of freedom. It is
to be hoped that this lesson, showing us as it does how much of
conscience and even of personal sincerity can co-exist with a
minimum of effective morality in international undertakings,
will some day be once more remembered; so that when our
nation is another time about to serve the devil do so with more
frankness and will deceive itself less by half-conscious cant. For
the rest, our mission in the cause of liberty is to be accomp-
lished through a steadfast devotion to the cause of our own
inner life, and not by going abroad as missionaries, as conquer-
ors or as marauders, among weaker peoples."

Josiah Royce, 1886
American Philosopher

Introduction

Since the United States is a global power with diverse commitments,
framers of policy towards any region must distinguish vital interests
from peripheral ones, the necessary from the desirable. A sense of
proportion is particularly germane when considering the small nations of
Central America and the Caribbean.[1] The central U.S. interests in the
region are:

1. protection of our national security
2. peace and stability
3. development with greater equity
4. furtherance of democracy and human rights

Economic Interests and National Security

The first priority of U.S. foreign and military policy is to secure the land, people and institutions of the United States at home. Our security does not depend on policing the globe against communism, however opposed to such ideology one may be. The conflict in Vietnam revealed the danger of committing U.S. lives and resources to a struggle that was not critical to our national security. To avoid repeating such a costly error, it is necessary to evaluate the threat posed by the struggles in Central America to our economic well-being and to our military security. Special interests should not be construed as the national interest.

U.S. banks and corporations have significant interests in the Caribbean and Central America which can be divided into three major areas: corporate investment and subcontracting, trade with or through the region, and bank loans.[2]

U.S. direct investment in the region totalled $20.8 billion in 1981, over 9 percent of the total U.S. investment abroad.[3] Less than one fourth of this was in Central America, the remainder in the islands of the Caribbean. In peacetime, 44 percent of all foreign cargo tonnage and 45 percent of the crude oil imported into the United States pass through the Caribbean. Only a minor share of this trade originates in countries of the region themselves. Just over two percent of U.S. trade is with the Caribbean nations, and only one percent with Central America. Two strategically important resources are supplied by the Caribbean: 85 percent of imported bauxite and 70 percent of imported refined petroleum.[4]

U.S. bank exposure in the region is of relatively greater significance primarily because the islands of the Caribbean provide off-shore banking platforms with minimal regulations or taxation. Excluding the capital residing in these tax shelters, approximately $2.3 billion was owed to U.S. banks by other countries in the region in 1982.[5]

The U.S. economy is also affected by the flow of refugees from the region. Estimates of undocumented immigrant aliens currently in the United States range from 3.5 to 6 million, the vast majority of them coming from Mexico, Central America and the Caribbean.[6] These immigrants form an easily exploited, low-wage labor pool which can have a significant impact on wages and unions in the United States.

While U.S. economic ties with the region are extensive, their importance should not be exaggerated. U.S. investments are significant but not vital to our economy. Other sources are available for the resources supplied by the region.

Moreover, none of these interests need be threatened by social change in the region. If Nicaragua is any example, post-revolutionary regimes can be expected to seek trade and aid from the United States. U.S. business investments will be protected or fairly compensated if nationalized. U.S. bank loans will be honored. The Nicaraguan government agreed to repay loans granted to the Somoza dictatorship in its last days, even though most of the money flowed into private bank accounts outside the country.[7] No country in the region can afford to risk economic isolation from the United States and the significant regional actors, Mexico, Colombia, and Venezuela.[8]

The United States' economic stake in the region must also be contrasted with its far more serious interests in the rest of the hemisphere. U.S. direct investment in Mexico alone totals about seven times that in all the countries of Central America (excluding Panama).[9] Mexico, Argentina, Chile and Brazil cover three quarters of Latin America's territory, and have three quarters of its population and its production. The outcome of the struggle in El Salvador or Guatemala is of minor importance compared to the crisis posed by the debt burden in these four countries. In each, austerity measures have dramatically increased deprivation and unrest with political upheaval a possible result. At stake is not only the internal stability of major nations in the hemisphere, but—without exaggeration—the fate of major American banks, and quite possibly the survival of the international monetary system. This is the true challenge to U.S. economic well-being in Latin America.

Geographic proximity invests events in Central America and the Caribbean with potential military significance. Obviously, the countries of the region themselves pose no intrinsic military threat to the United States. It is the assumption of expanding Soviet or Cuban presence that provides the basis for alarm. The principal threat is usually described as the prospect that a radical government may establish a military alliance with the Soviet Union, providing a base from which it could threaten vital sea lanes or launch a direct attack on the United States.

The actual threat posed by this hypothetical situation is negligible. In peacetime, the United States cannot under international law deny the Soviet Union access to the region's waterways.

The supposed conventional threat is based upon an implausible scenario. Any attack on the sea lanes, the Panama Canal or regional oil fields would be a clear act of war and would call forth an appropriate military response from the United States and its allies. Attacks on such targets make no military sense except in the context of a larger war between the United States and the Soviet Union, perhaps in Europe or the Middle East. One must assume that such a war remains *non-nuclear*; otherwise, the sea lanes of the Caribbean become irrelevant.

The United States has the capacity to destroy quickly the ability of any Central American regime to launch such military actions.[10] Therefore, a local regime would have to be prepared to commit suicide in order to give the Soviet Union a temporary advantage in a global conventional war with the United States. All of this strains credulity. It makes little sense for the United States to base its policy toward Central America on such unlikely developments.

Finally, this scenario also depends on Soviet willingness to take on the burden of financing Central American economies—presumably the *quid pro quo* for access to basing facilities—in order to obtain a posture it already possesses through its alliance with Cuba. The increased advantage of obtaining a similar ally in Central America is marginal.

The Cuban experience is illustrative. For nearly 25 years, the Soviet Union has supplied the Cubans with military aid, arms and training. Today, Cuba poses no significant military threat to the United States. By U.S. standards, its navy is miniscule; its air force is limited. The major foreign military base in Cuba is the U.S. base at Guantanamo. In 25 years of hostility between the United States and Cuba, Castro has not attempted to interfere militarily with any U.S. shipping or military activity. Most recently, the Cuban president informed the Nicaraguans that Cuba could not come to their defense in the event of an attack by the United States.[11]

Warnings about a Soviet military threat in Central America are essentially a distraction from more basic concerns. Neither the Nicaraguan government nor the revolutionary movements in El Salvador or Guatemala has expressed any interest in providing bases to the Soviet Union. Nor has the U.S.S.R. demonstrated any interest in bearing the economic and political burdens associated with acquiring and sustaining even a single such base. As McGeorge Bundy, former national security advisor to President Kennedy, has observed: "The realities of relative strength make it totally clear that no one is going to make war on us from Central America. There is something genuinely zany in thinking about the area in such terms."[12]

Another central security danger to the United States said to be posed by radical states in the region is that they will destabilize their neighbors, either by direct military threat or indirectly—by exporting revolution and allowing an expanded Cuban and Soviet presence in the region. Radical states, particularly those concerned about the hostility of the United States or their neighbors, are likely to seek and gain assistance in building up their armed forces, either from European countries or from the Soviet Union and Cuba. This build-up can in turn be said to pose a threat to their neighbors. Thus the Sandinista government is seen as mounting a direct military threat to Honduras and Costa Rica.[13]

But this threat is remote at best. The United States and the other leading actors in the region would come to the aid of any country under direct attack, and the Rio Treaty of Reciprocal Security Assistance provides an appropriate mechanism for response. U.S. officials admit privately that there is very little chance that the Sandinistas would invite their own destruction by striking across their borders. To date, even the launching of attacks by "contras" from Costa Rica and Honduras has not triggered a Nicaraguan response.[14]

The export-of-revolution theory comes in both simplistic and sophisticated variants. The simplistic version holds that external subversion is the source of internal insurrection, part of a Soviet–Cuban strategic plan to weaken the United States, and that were it not for the actions of Cuba and Nicaragua there would be no serious internal conflict in El Salvador. Today, the argument is also applied to alleged Nicaraguan efforts to destabilize Costa Rica and Honduras.[15]

The more elegant version holds that while internal conflict may be caused by long-term social, economic and political grievances, revolutionary victories in one country inspire revolutionary actions in another, whereas revolutionary defeats would discourage them.[16] Moreover, even internally generated insurrections require outside assistance to succeed. Thus Nicaragua is said to provide "essential support" to the guerrillas in El Salvador.[17] Without training and aid from Cuba and Nicaragua, the government could defeat the revolution in El Salvador and limit the spread of Soviet influence.

The United States and other governments in the region have every reason to be concerned about the export of violence from one country to another. Collective self-defense measures such as those suggested by the Contadora nations offer a proper response. The current alarm about the spread of Soviet influence through subversion grossly distorts the problem, however.

First, the triumph of a revolution need not result in a victory for the Soviet Union. In this hemisphere, fear of U.S. intervention often leads radical governments to seek ties with the Soviet Union and Cuba. But any post-revolutionary government faces a severe reconstruction challenge.[18] The central source of aid, trade and investment will necessarily be countries of the West—Europe, the United States and the rest of the hemisphere.[19] The Soviet Union, for example, has demonstrated little interest in or capacity for providing Nicaragua with the credits desperately needed for post-war reconstruction. The vast bulk of Nicaraguan assistance and trade comes from the West.

Second, while guns can be exported, revolution cannot. It is necessarily an indigenous process. The experience of Che Guevara in Bolivia in 1967 is dramatic testimony to the inability of "professional guerrillas" to export revolution, even to a country marked by injustice and poverty. Even administration spokesmen generally concede that in Nicaragua, El Salvador and Guatemala, the roots of the upheaval lie in entrenched inequality and human desperation combined with political repression that has erased any hope for nonviolent reform. The coalitions supporting the revolutions in Nicaragua and El Salvador are broad-based, with strong relations to popular organizations. If Cuba and Nicaragua were to disappear, the struggle in El Salvador would continue.

The spread of revolution is viewed by some as a threat to the United States because it might eventually engulf Mexico or Panama—two countries in which the United States has major strategic interests. But the greater threat to the people of those nations comes not from revolutions in neighboring countries, but from the potential regionalization of the war that may be the result of U.S. efforts to counter local upheavals. A regional war would increase the flood of refugees, and take an immense toll in lives and resources. It would be a cruel irony, indeed, if in preparing to counter revolutions that do not threaten our security, the United States sparked a regional conflict that could affect our interest directly. It is this very concern which has led Mexican leaders to seek a regional process of mediation to limit the current conflicts.

The disproportionate concern generated by the crisis in Central America grows out of the view that the prevention of "Marxist" regimes in the U.S. "backyard" is a test of American credibility throughout the world. In the president's April 1983 speech to Congress, the credibility stakes were clearly defined.

"If Central America were to fall, what would the consequences be for our position in Asia and Europe and for alliances such as NATO? If the United States cannot respond to a threat near our own borders, why should Europeans and Asians believe we are seriously concerned about threats to them?...The national security of all the Americas is at stake in Central America. If we cannot defend ourselves there, we cannot expect to prevail elsewhere. Our credibility would collapse, our alliances would crumble..."[20]

This language, reminiscent of the Johnson and Kissinger defense of the war in Vietnam, abstracts the crisis from real U.S. interests.[21] In this view, because Central America is in our "sphere of influence," the United States must demonstrate that it has the political will and ability to control events in the region. It matters little what the Sandinista government or the FDR–FMLN do; their mere existence becomes a perceived challenge to the United States. By this logic, the victory of a revolution or survival of a regime labelled Marxist, even if non-aligned, is intolerable for it will be perceived in Moscow, in Bonn, in Manila and in Riyadh as a sign of weakness.

The enhanced credibility which the administration seeks seems strangely divorced from reality. Key U.S. allies—Mexico, Venezuela and even Brazil—have clearly stated their opposition to U.S. military intervention in Central America.

Similarly, in Europe where popular opinion has already been shaken by the debate over deployment of cruise and Pershing missiles, it is clear that no leader would support U.S. intervention, as the condemnation of the Grenada invasion by Reagan's closest ideological ally, Margaret Thatcher, illustrates. U.S. intervention in Central America would also be universally condemned by the leaders of independent Third World countries. In fact, true concern for U.S. credibility throughout the world counsels prudence in the use of military force.

U.S. global commitments can only be sustained if they are regarded as legitimate by allies abroad and citizens at home. To maintain its leadership in the world, particularly the support of its European allies, the United States must exercise its power not in an uncritical defense of the status quo, but in defense of the right of other peoples to choose their own future—even when we may disagree with their choice.

The United States must use its overwhelming power with a sense of prudence and proportion. The war in Vietnam demonstrated clearly the cost to our credibility of defining U.S. interests recklessly and using military power imprudently. In Vietnam, a similar desire to demonstrate credibility led the U.S. government into a costly war that sapped its legitimacy at home and abroad, calling its global leadership into serious question. Even today, the political reverberations of Vietnam echo in Western Europe.

The Reagan administration may well fear the effect of the "loss" of El Salvador not upon the opinions of our democratic allies, but upon the leaders of unpopular governments throughout the world. The relevant audiences may not be Bonn or Mexico City, but Seoul and Manila. The fall of the government in El Salvador, it is claimed, would erode the credibility of U.S. pledges to support those leaders. But this "demonstration effect," to the extent that it operates, should not necessarily be discouraged. The United States should make it clear that there are no legal or moral obligations that require it to defend a government against its own people. If unpopular regimes around the globe rest assured that the United States will sustain them in the name of anti-communism, they have no incentive to seek greater domestic legitimacy through long-term reform. And by resisting reform, they hasten the day of their own demise. We should not mislead dictatorial regimes about U.S. capabilities and intentions, for it is not in the U.S. interest nor does the United States have the capability to defend dictatorships against internal upheaval.

The pursuit of credibility abroad also plays to another audience, the American citizenry. Too often, popular disapproval of prolonged military intervention—demonstrated repeatedly in polls—leads to campaigns designed to make the case for intervention, in Dean Acheson's words, "clearer than the truth."[22] Rhetoric escalates in the hope that hyperbole can convince the public that the stakes are "worth it."

But in a democracy, exaggerated government claims and efforts at deception do not go unexposed for long. The result, ironically, is a "credibility gap," which the Reagan administration has already begun to suffer in its Central America policy.

By themselves the revolutions in Central America are, at best, of marginal concern to our core national security, and the upheaval is less important than our reaction to it. A policy of intervention—even if successful—may pose a greater threat to our security by distracting us from more serious concerns and sparking significant opposition at home and abroad—than any revolution in Central America.

Peace and Stability

The United States has a broad long-term interest in peace and stability in the region. Violent upheaval is against U.S. interests, even if it does not threaten basic security. The cost in human casualties, economic disruption and physical destruction increases misery in the region. The flight of refugees and capital from the countries involved has detrimental economic effects. If a war becomes regionalized, even core U.S. security interests may come into play.

The critical challenge in Central America is how to respond to violent social revolution directed against governments that support U.S. foreign policy but sponsor internal repression. The general U.S. response has been to support the regime under challenge, increase military and economic assistance and encourage political and economic reforms in the midst of the war. Our fear of change leads us to embrace even the most unseemly and illegitimate regimes. U.S. security assistance bolsters the very forces most resistant to change. The clear U.S. national commitment to their survival removes any incentive for reforms that might reduce their privilege. The result is that ever greater U.S. commitment is needed to support an ever more hollow regime. In the end, direct intervention may become the only way to stave off ignominious failure.

The impunity with which death squads operate in El Salvador illustrates this dangerous cycle.[23] The murders of union leaders, peasants claiming their lands in the land reform program, priests and nuns aiding the poor, UNESCO teachers spreading literacy are not isolated excesses of ill-trained troops. They are part of a calculated, effective program to limit any reforms in order to secure the privileges of the elite. U.S. protestations about human rights have produced no effective response. Since the United States has defined its national security goal as requiring the crushing of the revolutionary challenge in El Salvador, the right-wing government there is confident that the United States will not abandon it no matter what it does.[24]

Even if the United States were to succeed in defeating indigenous revolutionary movements by bolstering repressive regimes, the result is likely to be neither long-term stability, nor the professed goal of gradual reform. There is little precedent for elites to accept reforms that destroy their privileges, particularly after the revolutionary threat has been overcome. This was the lesson of the Alliance for Progress in Central America, under which counterinsurgency assistance was provided as a shield for reform and development. The existing elites gladly accepted the military and economic aid, defeated the embryonic guerrilla movements that sprouted in the wake of the Cuban revolution and then ignored or resisted U.S. efforts to promote reform. Once the revolutionary threat (whether real or not) had passed, both the existing elites and the United States quickly lost interest in reform. In Central America, there are no better examples than Guatemala and El Salvador. Ultimately, the product of the strategy is perpetual instability, for the grievances that gave rise to the revolution, if unattended, give rise to it again and again.[25]

A longer-term policy would seek good relations with the peoples of the region, rather than frozen commitments to any one regime. Diversity and self-determination should be accepted, even encouraged. Conflict should be localized through collective efforts to limit external intervention. By acting to limit the violence rather than to fuel it, by distancing the United States from a regime under attack by its own people, by offering the good offices of the United States for a negotiated settlement, U.S. policy can better serve its long-term interest in good relations and stability.

Economic Development with Equity

The United States has a direct interest in equitable economic development in the region. Development increases opportunities for trade and investment, directly benefitting the U.S. economy. Fairer distribution of resources would not only expand internal markets, but decrease the disparity between labor costs in the United States and those in the region. This in turn would diminish the flow of refugees into the United States and the flight of jobs from it.

Development with equity is vital if stability is to be achieved. In societies with extreme disparities in wealth and income, policies that produce growth in gross national product may benefit only the wealthy few and ignore the plight of the many.

An end to conflict, however, is a prior condition for genuine economic development. Without peace, economic assistance becomes subordinated to military purposes. In El Salvador, aid provided as Economic Support Funds becomes the hard currency necessary for the government to continue its military build-up.[26] Whatever development effect it has is more than countered by the flight of capital and the destruction of infrastructure—bridges, dams, roads—in the fighting.

Thus the United States has a direct interest in cooperating in a long-term development plan for the region. To succeed, the plan must build upon a peace not made and dominated by the United States, but forged within and between the countries of the region. It must be an instrument of unity rather than division. It must also be specifically designed to encourage more equitable distribution of resources and the development of democratic institutions rather than simply to reinforce current patterns of inequality.

Domestic Values: Democracy and Human Rights

It is in the direct interest of the United States to pursue policies that reflect and further our national values. Such an approach helps to insure popular support necessary to sustain a consistent policy toward our neighbors. It suggests principles that can guide the development of stable relations with countries in the region and promote long-term stability and peace.

In this hemisphere where our disparate power enables us to affect our will at minimal cost, we will also have to live with the legacy of past actions. The 1954 CIA-backed coup in Guatemala demonstrates the horror of ill-conceived short-term "successes." The military regime installed in 1954 has perpetuated itself since, wreaking havoc on Guatemala's economy. To sustain itself, it has pursued a genocidal war against the indigenous Indian population.[27] Today Guatemala stands, a pariah among nations, a tragic illustration of the consequences of a "successful" U.S. military intervention.

Principles for a New Policy

A realistic assessment of U.S. interests suggests a set of principles that reflect the values the United States wishes to represent in the world. Principles are not recipes for policy. They can be, and frequently are, bent to serve quite different policy objectives. But, taken together, the following seven principles provide a framework for a secure, stable relationship between the United States and Central America that can serve the interests of the American people and the people of the hemisphere.

Non-Intervention

The principle of non-intervention is part of U.S. law, incorporated in treaties and espoused in countless policy statements.[28] It is founded upon an essential recognition of the equality of sovereign states. The injunction to exercise self-restraint is of special relevance in the hemisphere where our overwhelming military and economic preponderance can be a temptation to intervention.

Claims that the principle of military non-intervention suggests a new isolationist policy are off point. The influence of the United States is not exercised solely—or even most effectively—through the barrel of a gun. As the central source of aid, trade and investment in the region, the United States possesses vast formal and informal resources with which it can exercise influence.

Nor does the principle of non-intervention require that the United States sit passively while our allies suffer external attack. Under the Rio Treaty of 1947 and the United Nations Charter, the United States is committed and entitled to act with its allies in collective self-defense against external attack. The entitlement is not a blank check, however. The arming and direction of private armies seeking to overthrow the sovereign government of Nicaragua violates these agreements.

Self-Determination

Respect for self-determination is a corollary of non-intervention. The people of each nation have the right to determine the political and social system under which they will live.[29] The United States should endorse diversity in the region. Indeed, it is the violation of the right to self-determination by the Soviet Union in Eastern Europe that earns it condemnation. Repeated past violations of the principle of self-determination by the United States in this hemisphere offend nationalist sentiments everywhere.

Respect for the principle of self-determination may save the United States from continued conflict with revolutionary movements and governments. Change is an inevitable part of history. Against repressive governments, violent change may be the only avenue available. The United States must come to terms with nationalist revolutions or be condemned to repeat costly and unpopular interventions.

Respect for self-determination requires that the United States be open to divergent economic and political experiences. We should be less quick to pin labels like "Marxist–Leninist" on radical regimes and more tolerant of experimentation with a variety of political and economic models.

At the same time, respect for self-determination does not prohibit the United States from expressing its preferences in its policies. While the expression of human rights concerns, for example, may constitute a theoretical infringement on the principle of self-determination, it does not violate the intent behind that principle. It is quite different when the United States speaks on behalf of oppressed people, using a single standard for all governments, than when it intervenes on behalf of U.S. special interests or because of geo-political fears.

Collective Self-Defense

The United States should pursue its policies through multilateral consultations and abide by its pledge through the Organization of American States (OAS) to collective defense efforts.[30] Collective action recognizes the increasing influence of countries in the region like Mexico and Venezuela. U.S. policies simply cannot succeed without support from these countries and our European allies.

Consultation with independent allies can help correct our misconceptions about a situation, as exemplified by the mediation attempts of the Contadora nations in Central America. They can help us avoid unilateral intervention with the accompanying cost of regional hostility. Already our policy toward Nicaragua has caused Latin Americans to begin talking about organizing international brigades to fight U.S. intervention in Nicaragua.

Peaceful Settlement of Disputes

Diplomacy and mediation are powerful tools in the hands of a country of such economic and military power as the United States. It is a far superior instrument than arms or military intervention, if the objective is—as it should be—to promote peace and democracy in the region.

By seeking the peaceful resolution of disputes, the United States would also avoid the increasing costs of intervention. Even the invasion of tiny Grenada took a toll of 18 U.S. lives.[31] Intervention in Central America would be far more costly than it was in the 1920s and 1950s, both in lives and in political legitimacy.

Encouragement of Human Rights and Democracy

Both self-interest and principle counsel U.S. support for human rights and democratic institutions. Respect for the full range of human rights—

economic and social, as well as political and civil—is a precondition for legitimate governments open to change. It is vital that the United States not trivialize these concerns. Elections do not make democracy in societies dominated by security forces and death squads. Civil rights are undermined if basic human needs are denied to the mass of the population.

At the same time, support for human rights and democracy ought not produce shrill condemnation of governments seeking to meet the needs of their people. U.S. policy should be tolerant of different forms of participation and supportive of experimentation with a variety of democratic forms that conform to the special historical circumstances which better meet the needs of the people of the region than transplanted U.S. institutions. Above all, the United States should be prepared to allow governments in the region to make their own mistakes just as all sovereign nations, including our own, do. When these mistakes constitute a violation of human rights as defined by international law and treaties, we should consult with the other nations of the region and take appropriate action together.

Domestic Legitimacy

United States foreign policy must be compatible with domestic values, priorities and responsibilities in order to sustain popular support. This report has suggested that events in the region touch U.S. interests at many points—employment, immigration, trade, and investment. One of the reasons that popular opposition to the administration policy is so great is that it is virtually impossible to argue convincingly that these policies further the interests of the majority of Americans. No easily identifiable business interests, except armaments manufacturers, no workers, except those in military related employment, are helped. The massive diversion of resources from human needs at home, to military commitments in Central America, exacerbates the suffering of women, minorities, and the unemployed.

In the last two decades the civil rights movement, the women's movement and the anti-nuclear campaign have brought new voices to the political dialogue. No longer can a small handful of unaccountable national security "experts" speak for the country on the most vital issues affecting our national survival. These new actors in the United States represent a different conception of American priorities. The so-called "gender gap" offers a glimpse of what is happening; a growing number of women have come to believe that issues of war and peace are too important to be left to a government composed, at its highest levels, almost entirely of men. Policies that grow out of traditional "bipartisan" cold war perspectives now face significant popular challenge.

Support for Equity and Development

U.S. economic assistance should be geared to promote both equity and development. Aid programs are too frequently viewed as instruments to reward friends and punish enemies in order to serve some overarching geo-political goal of the United States. But the economic development of U.S. neighbors is vital to the stability of the hemisphere, which should be a prime objective of U.S. policy in the region. The test for aid recipients should not be their ideology, but an objective assessment of what use they will make of the aid. Any government that can demonstrate commitment and competence in meeting basic human needs such as literacy and health should receive support for its efforts. Wherever possible, U.S. aid should encourage regional development and integration.

This does not require abandonment of bilateral aid programs. But it is not in the U.S. interest to provide aid to governments engaged in a consistent pattern of gross violation of human rights, for in such situations, equitable development is not achievable. Regimes like that in Guatemala should be quarantined. Even in such situations, however, assistance can still flow to citizen organizations, to churches, to women's groups, and to grassroots organizations for the promotion of human rights.

Similarly, aid should be focused on countries where it can foster development. Countries which have a credible development plan for promoting basic human needs should be preferred recipients. Countries without such plans should be encouraged to develop them. For El Salvador, in the midst of a revolution, economic assistance is not development aid, but part of the military struggle, and should be considered as such.

56

Notes

1. Nicaragua, El Salvador and Guatemala combined are about the size of Oregon, and the per capita income of the region averages less than $800. See World Bank, *World Development Report 1983*, New York: Oxford University Press, July 1983, pp. 148-149.
2. See Appendix I for more complete description.
3. Calculated from Obie G. Whichard, "U.S. Direct Investment Abroad in 1982," *Survey of Current Business*, August 1983, p. 23. The Netherlands Antilles are excluded from the figures because billions of dollars show up in U.S. corporate affiliates there to escape U.S. withholding taxes on interest payments to foreigners. Of the $20.8 billion total, $4.8 billion was in Central America, and $16.0 billion was in the Caribbean.
4. Calculated from data in United States, U.S. Department of Commerce, Bureau of Census *Highlights of U.S. Export and Import Trade*. FT990, Washington, D.C.: Government Printing Office, December 1982, pp. 32, 72.
5. Estimated by INIES/CRIES, quoted in Mark Hansen, "U.S. Banks in the Caribbean: Towards a Strategy for Facilitating Lending to Nations Pursuing Alternative Models of Development," paper prepared for PACCA, October 1983, p. 5.
6. J. Vialet, "Immigration Issues and Legislation in the 98th Congress," Issue Brief No. 1B83087 (Washington, D.C.: Library of Congress, Congressional Research Service, October 14, 1983), p. 5.
7. In May 1979, the International Monetary Fund (IMF) awarded the Somoza government a $66 million credit. By June 1, the first half of the loan had been deposited in the Central Bank in Managua. But following the Sandinista takeover in July, officials found only $3.5 million in the Bank's reserves. See *Washington Post*, July 26, 1979.
8. For example, see Junta of the Government of National Reconstruction, *The Philosophy and Policies of the Government of Nicaragua* (Managua: Direccion de Divulgacion y Prensa, March 1982), pp. 2-5.
9. In 1981, U.S. direct foreign investment in Mexico totaled $7.0 billion; in Panama, $3.8 billion; and in the rest of Central America, $1.0 billion. See Whichard, *op. cit.*, p. 23.
10. As the former Commander of the U.S. Southern Command, General Wallace Nutting, has noted, "In a geographical sense, at least, the Central America-Caribbean basin area is our Afghanistan, and if push comes to shove in this region, the outcome is not in doubt. It would be very difficult for the Soviet Union to project the kind of conventional power into the Caribbean Basin that we can't deal with." See *U.S. News and World Report*, June 13, 1983, pp. 25-26.
11. "Fidel Castro's Press Conference on Grenada," *Foreign Broadcast Information Service: Latin America*, October 26, 1983, p. Q14.
12. *New York Times*, January 6, 1984.
13. Undersecretary of Defense Fred Ikle describes the Nicaraguan military threat: "The Sandinista Regime is determined to create a 'second Cuba' in Central America. Ever since they seized power, the Sandinistas embarked on a major military buildup. Today, they have a much larger army than Somoza ever had, and they have expressed the intention to build the largest force in Central America. Nicaragua is building new military airfields, and is importing Soviet tanks, helicopters, armored vehicles and other equipment. The 'second Cuba' in Nicaragua would be more dangerous than Castro's Cuba since it shares hard to defend borders with Honduras and Costa Rica." See Speech by Fred Ikle, Baltimore Council on Foreign Affairs, Baltimore, Maryland, September 12, 1983. The relative strength of Honduras' armed forces was more clearly outlined in testimony given before the House Subcommittee

on Western Hemisphere Affairs on September 21, 1982, by retired Lt. Col. John H. Buchanan, USMC. He argued that the armed forces of Honduras and Nicaragua "have different areas of strength and weakness but the overall effect is a balance of force in the realm of more sophisticated weapons." Lt. Col. Buchanan concluded that a war between Honduras and Nicaragua "would truly be a 'war without winners'. . . Such a war could easily spark off a regional conflagration involving all the nations of Central America, and perhaps the U.S. and Mexico—on opposing sides." See Testimony of retired Lt. Col. John H. Buchanan, USMC, U.S. Congress, House Foreign Affairs Subcommittee on Inter-American Affairs, September 21, 1982. Quoted in Peter Rosset and John Vandermeer, eds., *The Nicaraguan Reader* (New York: Grove Press, 1983), pp. 55-57.

14. Nicaraguan soldiers guarding the border against incursions by anti-Sandinista rebels have returned fire against rebel targets in Honduras on several occasions. On January 11, 1984, a U.S. OH-58 helicopter apparently violated Nicaraguan airspace, took ground fire, and landed some 100 yards inside Honduras. Nicaraguan border guards reportedly continued firing on the helicopter, resulting in the death of an American officer. The helicopter's markings were obscured by mud, and it is the same model used by the contras to ferry supplies into Nicaragua. As of this writing, Reagan administration officials were still investigating why the aircraft ended up about 28 miles off course. See *Washington Post*, January 13, 1984.

15. U.S. Departments of State and Defense. *Background Paper: Central America*, Washington, D.C.: Government Printing Office, May 27, 1983.

16. "Right now, the countries of this hemisphere are facing an unprecendented communist offensive, an offensive which takes advantage of those [economic and political] conditions we seek to address. The American people must clearly understand the nature of this offensive. The Soviet Union, taking advantage of the opportunities it sees, and using Cuba and now Nicaragua as its proxies, has targeted Central America and the Caribbean. Communist penetration of this hemisphere presents a direct threat to the security interest of our country and of our friends." See Speech by Undersecretary of Defense, Nestor Sanchez, "The Situation in Central America and the Caribbean and U.S. policy," Charlottesville, Virginia, October 15, 1983.

17. Ikle, *op. cit.* For other views, see footnote 42 in Section 1.

18. The war in Nicaragua was extremely costly. According to the World Bank, direct damage to physical structures, equipment and inventories amounted to approximately $250 million. Capital flight just prior to and during the war exceeded $500 million, and income foregone during 1978-1980 surpassed $2 billion. Quoted in World Bank, *Nicaragua: The Challenge of Reconstruction.* Washington: World Bank, October 9, 1981, p. 2. In addition, the Sandinista government inherited a $1.64 billion external debt from the Somoza regime, the highest per capita debt of any Latin American nation at that time. Somoza left only $3.5 million in reserves in the Central Bank. See George Black, *Triumph of the People: The Sandinista Revolution in Nicaragua* (London: Zed Press, 1981), p. 201. The human costs were also high: 40,000 dead, some 100,000 wounded, 40,000 children orphaned, 200,000 families left homeless, and 750,000 dependent on food assistance. See Center for International Policy, *Nicaragua: America's Second Chance*, International Policy Report, Vol 5, No. 5, Washington, D.C.: Center for International Policy, December, 1979, p. 6.

19. During the Sandinista government's first two-and-one-half years, it received 49 percent of its aid from other Third World nations, 32 percent from developed coutries, and 19 percent from the socialist countries, according to Nicaragua's International Fund for Reconstruction (FIR). Junta of the Government of National Reconstruction, *op. cit.*, p. 13.

20. Speech by Ronald Reagan to a Joint Session of Congress, Washington, D.C., April 27, 1983.

21. In a speech on Vietnam given at Johns Hopkins University in Baltimore, Maryland,

on April 7, 1965, President Lyndon Johnson said: "...we have made a national pledge to help South Vietnam defend its independence. And I intend to keep that promise. To dishonor that pledge, to abandon this small and brave nation to its enemies, and to the terror that must follow, would be an unforgivable wrong... Around the globe from Berlin to Thailand are people whose well being rest in part on the belief that they can count on us if they are attacked. To leave Vietnam to its fate would shake the confidence of all these people in the value of an American commitment and in the value of America's word. The result would be an increased unrest and instability, and even wider war." Henry Kissinger also often invoked global consequences of a U.S. defeat. "The United States," said Kissinger, "cannot accept a military defeat," in Vietnam; to do so would "unloose forces that would complicate prospects for international order." Quoted in Roger Morris, *Uncertain Greatness: Henry Kissinger and American Foreign Policy* (New York; Harper and Row, 1977), p. 152.

22. Quote from Dean Acheson, *Present at the Creation* (New York: W.W. Norton and Co., 1969), p. 375. In June 1983, in answer to the question, "To prevent a Communist overthrow of the government of El Salvador would you support sending U.S. combat forces to Central America?", fifty-six percent of the American people polled said "no," 32 percent said "yes," and 12 percent had "no opinion." See Press release, CBS/*New York Times* poll, July 1983. Following the October 1983 invasion of Grenada, 51 percent of the American people polled said they felt that President Reagan "uses the military too quickly" to solve international problems, and 34 percent indicated they felt he "uses diplomacy enough." Furthermore, 52 percent "feel uneasy about his approach" to crisis, and 39 percent say he "handles a crisis wisely." See CBS/*New York Times* poll, *New York Times*, October 29, 1983. In January 1984, 55 percent of the American people polled said they disapprove of U.S. efforts to overthrow the Nicaraguan government, 23 percent said they approve, and 22 percent had "no opinion." See *Washington Post/ABC News Poll, Washington Post*, January 20, 1984.

23. For an excellent discussion of El Salvador's death squads, see a series of articles by *Los Angeles Times* reporter Laurie Becklund (*Los Angeles Times*, December 18 and 19, 1983) and *Albuquerque Journal* reporter Craig Pyes (December 18, 19, 21 and 22, 1983).

    As described by Becklund and Pyes, the death squads are right-wing vigilante groups whose assassinations of union leaders, politicians, church figures, and other suspected "subversives" are aimed at terrorizing the population and preventing reform and negotiations with the FDR-FMLN.

    Salvadoran and U.S. government sources quoted by Becklund say the most notorious death squads—the Squadron of Death, the Secret Anti-Communist Army, and others—"may be run by as few as 25 to 50 powerful military officers and businessmen." Members, supporters, and financial backers of the death squads "hold key positions in El Salvador's court system, its media, several government ministries, and most important, the military." Off-duty soldiers and policemen, as well as hired civilians, carry out the murders of the "subversives," who are often targeted by the intelligence offices of the National Guard, National Police, and the Treasury Police.

    The death squads have received foreign assistance, report Becklund and Pyes. A "cadre" of Argentine secret police, former Guatemalan vice-president Mario Sandoval Alarcon, and French veterans of the Algerian Secret Army (OAS) trained civilians and military officers in counterinsurgency techniques in 1980. It was on land in Guatemala owned by Sandoval, a leader of the Latin American branch of the Taiwan-based World Anti-Communist League, that Argentine military advisers trained the first group of Nicaraguan counterrevolutionaries in 1981. *Miami Herald*, December 19, 1982.

    According to Becklund and Pyes, the death squads are part of a political-military network that was established by military officers and businessmen in the aftermath of the October 15, 1979 coup d'etat by the reformist officers who overthrew the regime of Gen. Carlos Humberto Romero.

The formation of the network was based on a counterinsurgency strategy that former counterintelligence specialist Roberto D'Aubuisson and many other officers had studied in Taiwan in the late seventies. It entailed the creation of a political structure to support military and paramilitary activities. In December 1980, D'Aubuisson, who also attended the International Police Academy in Washington and a U.S. military school in the Panama Canal Zone, organized such a political support group, the Broad National Front (FAN). In early 1981, right-wing activist Paul Weyrich and aides of Sen. Jesse Helms convinced D'Aubuisson to transform his front into a political party for the purpose of giving El Salvador's ultra-rightists more domestic and international legitimacy. D'Aubuisson and his allies founded the Nationalist Republican Alliance (ARENA party) in May 1981, adopting the Republican Party's 1980 platform and principles from more authoritarian nationalist parties, such as the German Nazis, as part of its creed. In the March 1982 elections, ARENA won 25 percent of the vote, making it the largest right-wing party in El Salvador. D'Aubuisson won the presidency of the country's Constituent Assembly and is given a good chance to win the presidential elections scheduled for March 25, 1984.

According to Pyes, ARENA "embraces local military officers, security-force operations and a broad vigilante network of civil defense units suspected of being used to eliminate the party's political opposition." ARENA may be linked "to a single countrywide death-squad network, consisting primarily of three loosely knit regional organizations which in total do not exceed 50 persons," Pyes writes, citing U.S. intelligence sources.

Americas Watch, a U.S.-based human rights monitoring group, says that between October 1979 and September 1983, the Salvadoran armed forces and right-wing death squads killed more than 37,000 Salvadorans. See Americas Watch. "Human Rights Update on Central America," Washington, D.C.: Americas Watch, October, 1983, p.3. For further discussion on death squads, see Christopher Dickey, "Behind the Death Squads," *The New Republic*, December 26, 1981.

24. According to the March 1, 1981 *Washington Post*, "conservative Salvadoran businessmen who clearly have sympathy and support of the Reagan administration are saying that negotiations are not necessary or desirable." *Newsweek* later quoted an "unidentified death squad member": "I know Reagan is one of us. He's going to put this country back on track, help the military gain power." See *Newsweek*, March 16, 1981. In November 1980, members of El Salvador's wealthiest families hosted parties in their homes to celebrate the electoral victory of Ronald Reagan. See *Albuquerque Journal*, December 22, 1983.

25. For elaboration, see Walter LaFeber, *Inevitable Revolutions* (New York: W.W. Norton, 1983), pp. 164-176.

26. Between 1980 and 1983, the United States provided $327 million from its Economic Support Fund (ESF) to the Salvadoran government. This assistance differs from military aid in the strict sense in that it is not intended to purchase weapons. Rather, it finances projects that will "enhance a nation's security"—for example, the building of bridges, roads, etc. In addition, these monies address emergency needs— for food, medical supplies, or balance of payments support.

27. Shortly after he seized power in a military coup in March 1982, then Guatemalan president General Efrain Rios Montt launched a counterinsurgency drive in the countryside whose goals were to eradicate leftist guerrillas quickly and to reassert the government's control over the Indian population. See Americas Watch, "Creating a Desolation and Calling It Peace: May 1983 Supplement to the Report on Human Rights in Guatemala," New York: Americas Watch, May, 1983, p. 9.

According to correspondent Allan Nairn, the tactics of Rios Montt's pacification strategy were forced labor or "civil patrols" used for road repair, surveillance, and military operations, and a "series of province-by-province sweeps by troops to clear the tiny mountain villages and to resettle much of the population in army-controlled towns." See "The Guns of Guatemala," *The New Republic*, April 11, 1983, p. 18. Indians comprise approximately 90-100 percent of the population where these sweeps occurred.

In June 1982, an unidentified western European diplomat based in Guatemala City said: "Indians are systematically being destroyed as a group" (*New York Times*, June 3, 1982). Rios Montt dismissed these reports. Guatemalan security forces do not always distinguish between innocent civilians and guerrillas, he acknowledged. "Look, the problem of war is not just a question of who is shooting. For each one who is shooting there are ten working behind him. Rios Montt's press secretary, Francisco Bianchi, added: "The guerrillas won over many Indian collaborators. Therefore, the Indians were subversives, right? And how do you fight subversion? Clearly, you had to kill Indians because they were collaborating with subversion. And then they say, 'You're massacring innocent people.' But they weren't innocent. They had sold out to subversion." See *New York Times*, July 20, 1982.

An investigative team that interviewed Guatemalan refugees in southern Mexico in August 1982 charged that the Rios Montt government was "seeking to destroy once and for all the Indian way of life." The team, which was sent by Survival International/USA, an Indian rights organization, said the government was forbidding Indians to speak in their language, confiscating their traditional clothing, relocating them in "strategic hamlets," and destroying the land from which they derive their livelihood. Craig Nelson, Kenneth Taylor, Janice Kruger, *Witness to Genocide: The Present Situation of Indians in Guatemala* (London: Survival International, 1983), pp. 13-14.

Amnesty International/USA documented the killings of 2,600 Guatemalans at the hands of government security forces between March 23 and July 30, 1982. (Press Release, Amnesty International/USA, Washington, D.C., October 12, 1982). In a letter to Amnesty International/USA disputing the credibility of its findings, Assistant Secretary for Inter-American Affairs Thomas Enders said that since March 23, "the government of Guatemala has committed itself to a new course and has made significant progress" in honoring human rights. *Letter*, September 15, 1982.

In December 1982, Rios Montt declared that, "300,000 Indians have now been organized into civilian self-defense units." See Press Release #01, Embassy of Guatemala, Washington, D.C., December 3, 1982. He met with President Reagan on December 5 in Honduras and after told reporters: "We have no scorched-earth policy. We have a policy of scorched Communists." See *New York Times*, December 6, 1982.

By May 1983, an estimated 70,000 to 100,000 Indians had fled to southern Mexico. Americas Watch, *op. cit.*, p. 7. Inside Guatemala there was massive dislocation, writes Nairn. "Today there are tens of thousands of Guatemalans roaming the mountainsides and living in the villages and camps who have lost husbands, wives, children, friends, and homes, and who carry with them graphic memories of a brutal encounter with the government." The consequence, says Nairn, is that, "neither Rios Montt nor the officers and politicians constantly plotting to replace him can expect ultimately to achieve a military victory" over the guerrillas. "They are more likely to find themselves on a downward spiral—having to kill more and more to stave off the consequences of the killing they have done before." Nairn, *op. cit.*, p. 21.

28. Article 18 of the Charter of the Organization of American States reads: "No State or group of States has the right to intervene, directly or indirectly, for any reason whatever, in the internal or external affairs of any other State. The foregoing principle prohibits not only armed force but also any other form of interference or

attempted threat against the personality of the State or against its political, economic, and cultural elements."

Article 19 of the Charter reads: "No State may use or encourage the use of coercive measures of an economic or political character in order to force the sovereign will of another State and obtain from it advantages of any kind." See General Secretariat of the Organization of American States, *Charter of the Organization of American States As Amended by the Protocol of Buenos Aires in 1967.* (Washington, D.C.: Organization of American States, 1967), p. 6.

29. Article 12 of the OAS Charter reads: "The political existence of the State is independent of recognition by other States. Even before being recognized, the State has the right to defend its integrity and independence, to provide for its preservation and prosperity, and consequently to organize itself as it sees fit, to legislate concerning its interests, to administer its services, and to determine the jurisdiction and competence of its courts. The exercise of these rights is limited only by the exercise of the rights of other States in accordance with international law." *Ibid.*, p. 5.

30. Article 27 of the Charter reads: "Every act of aggression by a State against the territorial integrity or the inviolability of the territory or against the sovereignty or political independence of an American State shall be considered an act of aggression against the other American States."

Article 28 of the Charter reads: "If the inviolability or the integrity of the territory or the sovereignty or political independence of any American State should be affected by an armed attack or by an act of aggression that is not an armed attack, or by an extracontinental conflict, or by a conflict between two or more American States, or by any other fact or situation that might endanger the peace of America, the American States, in furtherance of the principles of continental solidarity or collective self-defense, shall apply the measures and procedures established in the special treaties on the subject." *Ibid.*, pp. 7-8.

31. Those injured numbered 88. Telephone interview with Public Affairs Office, U.S. Department of Defense, January 11, 1984.

3

An Alternative Policy

> Our government is the potent, the omnipresent teacher. For
> good or for ill, it teaches the whole people by its example. If the
> government becomes a lawbreaker, it breeds contempt for the
> law; it invites every man to become a law unto himself; it
> invites anarchy.
>
> U.S. Supreme Court Justice Louis Brandeis

A Program for Peace

Over the past three years, U.S. policy has had the effect of aggravating conflicts in Central America instead of mitigating them. The immediate priority of U.S. policy must be to move back from the brink of the war that now threatens the entire region. The following is a set of concrete steps toward this end.

Nicaragua

The Reagan administration bears the primary responsibility for the war against Nicaragua. The *contra* forces operating against Nicaragua from base camps in Honduras and Costa Rica have been armed and trained by the United States. On several occasions, administration spokesmen, including the president himself, have implied that the interests of the United States require the removal of the current government of Nicaragua.[1]

The secret war does not exhaust the Administration's policy of hostility towards Nicaragua. It has been reinforced by a large scale military build-up in Honduras, including the indefinite deployment of U.S. combat forces under the pretext of military exercises. Finally, the United States has used its considerable leverage in the international financial community to enforce a credit embargo designed to strangle the war-torn Nicaraguan economy.[2]

The war against Nicaragua is both illegal and counterproductive. It exacerbates tensions between Nicaragua and its neighbors, fuels the regional arms race, and thereby increases the danger of regional conflict. It erodes civilian democratic institutions in Honduras, and places greater pressure on Costa Rica's financially strapped democracy. Within Nicaragua, it increases domestic polarization by identifying the internal opposition with the *contras*, and justifies limitations on political freedoms. With their nation under external attack, Nicaragua's leaders are forced to seek military aid. Successful U.S. efforts to deny them access to Western European arms markets leaves Nicaragua with no alternative but to turn to Cuba and the Soviet Union for military support.[3] Instead of encouraging the new government to remain outside the East–West conflict, U.S. policy forces it into that conflict. No country can long remain nonaligned if it is under attack by a superpower.

Although all of these activities represent a clear violation of the UN and OAS charters, the Reagan administration has justified its policy of hostility towards Nicaragua on the grounds that the United States seeks only to prevent Nicaragua from exporting revolution and endangering the security of its neighbors. But if the preservation and strengthening of democratic institutions is understood as an essential element of Costa Rican and Honduran security, then the security of these countries is today more endangered by their role as military staging areas for the war against Nicaragua than by anything Nicaragua itself has done.

Moreover, Nicaragua has offered to negotiate verifiable accords covering all the security concerns of its neighbors. It has made these offers bilaterally, multilaterally through the Contadora process, and has even offered similar negotiations to the United States.[4] As of January 1984, the United States has disparaged and dismissed all Nicaraguan initiatives.

If the real concern of the United States is that Nicaragua live in peace with its neighbors, now is the time for the United States to test the Nicaraguans' sincerity at the bargaining table.

A new policy towards Nicaragua must begin with the recognition that the 1979 revolution was an overwhelmingly popular insurrection against a hated dictatorship, and was supported by all sectors of Nicaraguan society. The way in which the domestic revolutionary process has unfolded subsequently, and how it proceeds in the future, is a matter for the Nicaraguan people to decide. This is a fundamental issue of self-determination.

The United States has every right to express its criticism of Nicaragua when internal developments there run contrary to our own values. But we do not have the right to dictate how Nicaraguans organize their own political and economic affairs—especially in view of the long support accorded to the corrupt and brutal Somoza dynasty by the United States.

The United States does, however, have a legitimate interest in how Nicaragua conducts relations with its neighbors. These are issues which can and should be addressed at the negotiating table.

A new policy toward Nicaragua should begin with the following practical steps:

1. Cease support for the paramilitary exile groups attacking Nicaragua from Honduras and Costa Rica, and discourage other nations from providing such support.
2. Cut back the military force the United States has assembled around Nicaragua, including an end to military exercises in Honduras and off the Nicaraguan coast, and the withdrawal of U.S. combat forces currently deployed in Honduras.
3. End the effort to strangle Nicaragua's economy by blocking international credits.
4. Fully support and encourage a negotiated reduction of tension and the normalization of relations between Nicaragua and Costa Rica and Honduras. Such negotiations can take place either bilaterally or under the auspices of the Contadora Group, but should follow the basic outlines of the security proposals made thus far under Contadora's auspices, and should include provisions for adequate verification of compliance. They should also include provisions for a humane resettlement plan for those who were recruited to fight the covert war.
5. Accept Nicaragua's offer to negotiate bilateral security concerns.

El Salvador

The origins of the current civil war in El Salvador are traceable to the early 1970s, when the oligarchy and its guardians in the Armed Forces responded to reformist demands for social and political change with brutal repression. Yet, the Reagan administration has held repeatedly that the war is fueled primarily by external interference from Nicaragua, Cuba and the Soviet Union.

This misperception of the war has led to a misprescription for policy. Because it sees the Salvadoran war largely in East–West terms, the Reagan administration has sought to resolve it militarily—by giving the Salvadoran Armed Forces the training and equipment to win the war. It is a policy which has failed dramatically. Despite their overwhelming advantages in air power, manpower and equipment, the Salvadoran army continues to lose the war.[5]

The Reagan administration has also tried to strengthen the Salvadoran regime politically by urging it to undertake a limited agrarian reform and to improve its abysmal human rights record. This too has failed to produce any significant results. Thus, the Reagan administration has vetoed legislation which would require it to certify progress in these areas.

No amount of military or economic assistance from the United States will stabilize the government of El Salvador or turn it into a democracy. The army of El Salvador fights poorly because the realities of Salvadoran society give the individual soldier little reason to fight. The government of El Salvador will not undertake reform because the oligarchy's unwillingness to tolerate even minimal reform is the root cause of the war in the first place.

A massive increase in military and economic aid from the United States will accomplish little more than to give an unsustainable regime the wherewithal to continue at unconscionable cost in human life. The 37,000 noncombatant civilians murdered by government forces and their affiliated death squads during the past four years do not represent an aberration or excess that U.S. pressure can alleviate; rather, they represent graphically the nature of the Salvadoran regime and its utter lack of legitimacy.[6] Since La Matanza ("the massacre") of 1932, the violent suppression of all types of dissent has been the normal operating procedure of the Salvadoran regime—a necessary condition for perpetuating itself in power.

The United States has publicly declared its support for democracy in El Salvador, but there can be no democracy and no truly free elections in the midst of the current violence. Elections, such as those conducted in 1982 or those scheduled for 1984, cannot resolve the basic conflicts of Salvadoran society.

If there is to be a political solution to the war in El Salvador, a solution short of military victory, it can only be achieved by negotiations. The Salvadoran government's offer to negotiate the terms on which the guerrillas lay down their arms and join elections controlled by the current regime and its security forces provides little more than the terms of surrender, an unlikely prospect since the guerrillas are winning the war.

Real negotiations in El Salvador—negotiations that actually have some chance of ending the war—must be aimed at creating an interim coalition government which is broadly based, has the confidence of all parties and will prepare genuinely free and fair elections under neutral international supervision. This is the sort of comprehensive political solution that the United States should seek in El Salvador. The alternatives are a continuing war, consuming ever greater quantities of resources from the United States—perhaps ultimately the lives of U.S. soldiers as well—or a guerrilla military victory.

To move towards a negotiated settlement of the Salvadoran civil war, the United States should:

1. Declare its unequivocal support for a political solution and seek a similar commitment from other countries in and near the region—particularly the Contadora group.
2. Suspend military assistance to the government of El Salvador and condition continued economic assistance upon the willingness of the government to enter into negotiations aimed at producing a cease-fire, the elimination of state terrorism from the security forces and death squads, and the establishment of a new interim government.
3. Seek the broadest possible group of international guarantors for the outcome of negotiations.
4. Take the lead in assembling a consortium of donor nations to provide reconstruction assistance to a new transitional government.

Honduras

The Reagan administration is converting Honduras into a forward military base of the United States. In the past few years, the United States has provided unprecedented quantities of military equipment to Honduras,[7] carried out extraordinary military exercises with the Honduran military, begun the construction of major military installations and urged Honduras to play a central role in the revival of the Central

American Defense Council (CONDECA), a regional organization for military cooperation that would now involve Honduras, Guatemala and El Salvador. This policy is directed towards the war against Nicaragua and the civil war in El Salvador. The United States is fashioning Honduras into a military instrument to support U.S. objectives in those other conflicts.

The consequences for Honduras have been tragic. The fragile elements of civil government in Honduras are crumbling before the process of militarization. A familiar spiral of repression has begun, "disappearances" and torture are mounting, and civilian opponents of the regime are increasingly intimidated.[8] The government has been diverted from solving deep-seated social and economic problems as its attention has been focused on the conflicts of its neighbors.

It is not in the interest of the United States to see Honduras engulfed by domestic turmoil or to have Honduras drawn into the conflicts of its neighbors. Nor is it in the U.S. interest to see Honduras' embryonic transition to democracy overwhelmed by the growing weight of the military in Honduran politics. Sadly, much of the distortion of Honduran political development which has occurred over the past three years has been a direct result of the policies of the United States, and only action by the United States can begin to reverse the trend. In order to accomplish this task, the United States should:

1. Withdraw U.S. military personnel from Honduras and dismantle the U.S. military installations and air bases currently under construction.
2. Offer strong support to those civilian political forces that are attempting to address the real development needs of what is still Central America's poorest country.
3. Take a strong pro-human rights stand before gross violations of human rights exceed the already unacceptable level.
4. Strongly urge Honduras to enter bilateral discussions with Nicaragua in an effort to alleviate border tensions and reduce the danger of war.

Guatemala

In human terms, Guatemala has suffered tragedy as deep as El Salvador's. From the middle 1950s through the 1970s, tens of thousands of Guatemalans were killed by the Armed Forces and death squads. Between 1966 and 1976 alone, 20,000 people were slain.[9] In the 1980 the level of repression has increased. From January to November 1980, some 3,000 people described by Guatemalan government representatives as "subversives" and "criminals" were either shot on the spot in political assassinations or seized and murdered later.[10] In October 1982, Amnesty International reported the deaths of 2,600 Guatemalans at the hands of the security forces from March through July 1982,[11] many of them Indians who were suspected of having guerrilla sympathies. Although there is no way to verify the statistics, most sources agree that between 5,000 and 8,000 persons were murdered in that year alone. Although the United States cannot by itself end this carnage, it should at a minimum do the following:

1. Maintain the suspension of all military and economic aid until there is a government that demonstrates its commitment to basic human rights.
2. Encourage Mexican attempts to deal with the growing Guatemalan refugee problem, funneling refugee aid through appropriate international and non-governmental organizations.
3. Take special cognizance in international and regional organizations and fora of the specific threat to indigenous populations and culture in Guatemala.

Costa Rica

Costa Rica is economically bankrupt; it is also the most long-lived and stable democracy in the region. The primary goal of the United States with respect to Costa Rica should thus be to help that financially troubled nation face its economic crisis, without at the same time undermining its political and social institutions. To that end, the United States should:

1. Stop all current U.S.-backed efforts to build a larger military establishment in Costa Rica.
2. Immediately withdraw support for Nicaraguan exiles using Costa Rica as a base for military attacks against the Sandinista regime.
3. Encourage negotiations between Costa Rica and Nicaragua to resolve any border disputes.

4. Cooperate both bilaterally and internationally with all those sectors of Costa Rican society genuinely committed to a democratic and equitable response to the current economic crisis. This implies a substantial commitment of bilateral and multilateral aid to Costa Rica.

The Caribbean

Although trade, debt and development problems are acute in the Caribbean, the islands other than Cuba are not intimately involved with the question of war and peace in Central America.

All recent U.S. administrations have insisted that Cuba is a key national security threat, and the Cubans themselves have openly said that they support the Nicaraguan revolution and the guerrilla struggles in El Salvador and Guatemala. The Cuban role, however, should not be exaggerated. Whatever the actual level of Cuban aid to the Nicaraguan revolution and to the insurgent movements, it is clear that the Castro government's role in the Central American crisis is not decisive. The crisis predated Cuban involvement by more than 30 years and as the former U.S. chargé d'affairs in Cuba Wayne Smith has written, it would continue even if Cuba were to disappear tomorrow.[12] Nevertheless, it is difficult to imagine a serious re-evaluation of the U.S. role in Central America that does not involve a re-evaluation of U.S.–Cuban relations.

Current policy lacks any rationale. The United States trades with the Soviet Union, seeks military cooperation with China, guarantees loans to communist countries in Eastern Europe and yet maintains an economic boycott of Cuba, an island 90 miles off our coast. The economic embargo has forced an unnatural Cuban economic and security dependence on the Soviet Union. Yet, it has failed to isolate Cuba internationally or to undermine the Cuban regime.

The United States should move towards normal relations with Cuba, thereby reasserting some of our political, economic and cultural influence. A necessary first step is to end the economic embargo, considered an act of war under international law. Normal relations at this point may not significantly decrease Cuban reliance on the Soviet Union, but they surely could not have worse results than the current policy which limits our influence without achieving our ends.

To begin the process of re-evaluation, the United States should:

1. Lift the economic boycott of Cuba and negotiate outstanding economic claims.
2. Begin negotiations on all outstanding bilateral concerns, including Cuban presence and activities in the region.
3. Encourage reintegration of Cuba into Latin America in general, and the Caribbean region in particular.

The 23 specific proposals listed above do not exhaust the steps that might be taken in the process of defining and putting into practice a new policy toward Central America and the Caribbean region as a whole. They do, however, suggest the kinds of steps that will have to be taken if U.S. policy is to serve U.S. interests and reflect our nation's principles. Furthermore, although not specifically mentioned as policy suggestions, it should be clear that this approach implies three substantial and crucial shifts in the way in which the United States thinks about and reacts to revolutionary upheavals, not only in this hemisphere, but elsewhere.

First, these policies assume that neither the Soviet Union nor the East–West struggle is at the center of the crisis—or, for that matter, at the center of a resolution of the crisis. Indeed, U.S. policy should seek to remove internal conflicts from an East–West context, not place them in it. Second, these policies suggest that new forms of participation and even democracy may issue from revolutionary turmoil. These will not necessarily be forms instantaneously recognizable to most citizens of the United States. Nevertheless, it is in the long-term interest of the United States to strive to understand that decades of exploitation and repression cannot always be fought with elections. Nor will the political forms that emerge in the region necessarily look like those that emerged in the United States in the 1780s—or, for that matter, in the 1980s. Finally, the policies advocated here imply that a major role will have to be played by other regional powers in the resolution of Central American conflicts. The increasing influence of regional powers, particularly Mexico and Venezuela, should be encouraged, providing a local context for mediating conflicts to which the United States is a party.

A Program for Development

Long term stability in Central America and the Caribbean depends on economic development that is based upon the needs of the majorities. U.S. aid, trade, investment and other forms of involvement can play a constructive role in this process.

But development is impossible in the midst of war. In El Salvador, for example, estimates suggest that over $1.2 billion have been taken out of the country in the last three years. The gross national product has decreased 25 percent. U.S. economic aid, totalling over $1 billion in the same period, has barely been able to keep the country functioning or to sustain its military build-up. When the fighting has ended, U.S. policies of aid, trade and investment should follow guidelines designed to encourage development and social justice.

The proposals below on aid and trade were formulated by The Development Group for Alternative Policies based on a conference of nongovernmental development organizations from the region.[13]

Aid

Two central guidelines should inform U.S. aid to the countries of the region:

—Government-to-government aid should be conditioned on serious plans to improve the lives of the poor. No longer should U.S. aid increase instability by benefiting the rich at the expense of the majority. Those countries with policies in place that narrow the income and poverty gaps between rich and poor should be favored in U.S. aid programs. Additional evidence of government concern for the poor are free functioning workers' organizations, community associations and other popular organizations.

—Government-to-government assistance should be open to diverse national experiments. Countries seeking to improve the lives of the poor should be eligible, even if their internal political structures do not meet with U.S. approval. Upon a diplomatic resolution of tensions between Nicaragua and its neighbors, Nicaragua should be eligible for aid.

In addition to these two central principles, aid to the region will be most effective if it respects the following guidelines:

The Building of Democratic Institutions

A major purpose of the economic assistance delivered by the United States to the countries of the region should be the strengthening of and, where necessary, support for the emergence of institutions which incorporate the poor in decision-making regarding resource allocation in their communities and at the national level. These institutions may be both public and private in nature, although in some countries funding would of necessity focus on non-governmental and popular organizations.

Promoting Regional Cooperation and Economic Integration

Cooperation among the countries of the region should be encouraged by the United States.

Financial and technical assistance should promote the diversification of local economic activity and further national and regional economic integration. Priority should be given to assisting small- and medium-scale indigenously-owned agro-industries in an effort to increase local food production and slow rural-urban migration. A priority should also be placed on projects which meet the particular needs of women. The United States should encourage the Central American republics to continue to complete the process of reorganizing the common market and its institutions, a process that has been substantially paralyzed by the wars. Such reorganization should be oriented towards promoting both economic and social development for the benefit of the majority of the population and not an elite of entrepreneurs.

Large assistance funds will permit the financing of large-scale projects, often on a regional basis, that usually cannot be carried out by any one country alone. A priority in this area should be the expansion of inter-island transportation and communications links in the Eastern Caribbean to help overcome some critical bottlenecks, particularly in the movements of goods in the region. Other areas of financing could include the exploration for and development of energy resources in the region, economic recovery and reconstruction in the aftermath of natural disasters and humanitarian assistance to the region's growing number of refugees.

Expanding Local Food Production

Support should be given to efforts to increase staple crop food production for domestic consumption, thus decreasing external dependence on food imports. Financing and technical assistance should be provided for integrated rural development projects involving: peasant family holdings; cooperatives and other organized groups; female-headed households; hydroagricultural improvement schemes using available water resources and appropriate technology; projects designed for crop protection, preservation, storage and marketing, as well as processing; fishery and fish-farming projects; and other endeavors aimed at providing incentives for increasing food production and at improving social and physical infrastructure to increase the viability of rural life.

Using Economic Support Funds (ESF) for Development Purposes

The United States should make available ESF financing to those countries in the Caribbean and Central America suffering from a scarcity of foreign exchange or requiring foreign currency to cover expected shortfalls during a period of economic or export diversification. Allocation of these monies—split in each case between grants and soft loans—should be based upon applications from the various nations outlining the need for the funds and the use to which they would be put. The principal purpose of ESF financing should not be to free the limited foreign exchange holdings of these countries for repayment to international commercial banks, but rather to help nations improve the plight of the majority of the population, including the poor and working classes, and to diversify their economies.

Implementing the Assistance Program

Development programs should receive assistance through those institutional channels that best promote democratic organizations, economic progress on an equitable basis and regional integration. The U.S. Agency for International Development should provide assistance to those governments which demonstrate their commitment to bridging the gap between rich and poor. The Inter-American Foundation and those American private voluntary organizations which also work to strengthen local indigenous institutions deserve continued support for their efforts on behalf of democratic, participatory development.

In addition to the U.S. government, U.S. corporations and banks should better respect the economic needs of host countries as expressed through national and regional development plans. New investment should involve local capital more in joint ventures aimed at producing for local markets. A recent survey revealing that U.S. corporations have 274 direct investments in 22 socialist countries suggests that corporations can indeed operate profitably within different social systems. The

United States should also practice non-discrimination in multilateral agencies.

Trade

The trade policy of the United States toward the region, like its aid program, should be designed to have a constructive impact upon the poorest people of Central America and the Caribbean. Unfortunately, the debate in this country on trade policy has been cast as a choice between free trade and protectionism. But the need is for a more innovative trading system that actually helps rather than hurts the poor.

Granting Duty-Free Treatment

All countries in the region, except those not seeking to bridge the gap between their rich and poor populations, should benefit from duty-free treatment for eligible articles[14] they directly export to the customs territory of the United States. In this context, measures which have restricted U.S. trade with Cuba and Nicaragua should be dropped.

Such duty-free treatment should be offered in order to stimulate the development of primarily small- and medium-sized indigenous manufacturing and agricultural enterprises capable of contributing to the foreign exchange earnings of their respective countries, as well as to domestic economic diversification and integration, while protecting worker health and safety,[15] the local food base and the environment.

Reserving Land and Other Natural Resources for Food Production

Duty-free treatment of sugar, syrups and molasses, beef and veal products, and other primary and related semi-processed goods from a Caribbean Basin country should be granted only upon that country's submission of an acceptable staple food protection plan. The purpose of the plan would be to ensure that present levels of domestic food production and the nutritional health of the population are not adversely affected by changes in land and marine resource use and alterations in land ownership caused by expanded production of these products in response to duty-free access to the U.S. market. This proposal was included in the Caribbean Basin Initiative at the insistence of several non-governmental organizations. We urge that it be implemented in the framework presented here.

Stabilizing Commodity Export Earnings

The overreliance of the countries in the region on one or two export commodities makes them particularly vulnerable to price fluctuations in world markets. Attempts to remedy the harmful effects of the instability of export earnings on the region's economies have left this problem unresolved. The European Economic Community did, however, take an important step toward the provision of at least partial and temporary relief for their former colonies with the implementation of a "STABEX" scheme.[16] The United States should establish a similar facility with the countries of the Basin.

Once established, the system would increase stability in earnings derived from exports to the United States of products upon which these economies are dependent and which are affected by fluctuations in price and/or quantity. These products include those primary and semi-processed goods which have suffered from a deterioration in the terms of trade between the country concerned and the United States and which meet the same criteria, where relevant, as those used to determine the eligibility of products for duty-free treatment. The specifics of such a system should be studied in detail, including the means to finance it.

Debt

Severe debt crises now plague the major countries of Latin America, including certain countries in Central America and the Caribbean. Between 1978 and 1982, the total external debt of Central America grew from $5.9 billion to $13.8 billion, or a 173 percent increase. Debt service as a share of Central American export earnings reached an alarming 28 percent by 1982, a level also approached by Jamaica, Haiti, the Dominican Republic and a growing number of Caribbean nations. Hence, many countries in Central America and the Caribbean have joined the club of major Third World debtors for whom the servicing of debt payments placed an enormous strain on economic resources.

The United States should approach this crisis as part of a global problem by shifting its entire policy on debt away from singular reliance on International Monetary Fund (IMF) austerity programs and short-term financing by commercial banks toward a different agenda.

In particular, the United States should play a leading role in international fora pursuing:

1. Long term (20-30 years), lower interest rescheduling of large parts of the $700 billion debt owed by the Third World, to be conducted under generally agreed rules for eligibility and negotiation, as well as common procedures.
2. Reorganization of the IMF, granting developing countries a larger share of quotas and creating a new low-conditionality, appropriate facility which would avoid the massive social dislocations of current adjustment programs.
3. The convening of a new international monetary conference to begin serious global debate on these and other pressing issues.

Domestic Economy

Development efforts in the hemisphere should be designed with concern for our domestic economy. Legislation should be passed to guarantee basic protection to American workers affected by the flow of goods and capital to and from the region. The United States should pursue a "full-trade" policy that encourages the exports of goods made by U.S. workers while curbing the export of jobs by U.S. multinationals.

In particular, support should be extended to:

1. Reductions in tax incentives that encourage U.S. companies to open plants overseas. These currently range from reductions on import duties for goods assembled abroad to tax credits and deductions for taxes paid to foreign governments.
2. Encouragement to U.S. corporations to create equal numbers of jobs at home when they set up shop overseas, to retrain laid-off workers, and to convert "runaway" plants for other uses.
3. Efforts by the AFL–CIO to generate legislation requiring information disclosure to workers well in advance of corporate plans to introduce labor cutting technology or to relocate elsewhere.

Such components of a domestic industrial policy could help to offset adverse effects that an "open" nonprotectionist trade policy may have on workers.

Immigrants and Refugees

Caribbean and Central American migration is believed to exercise a significant impact on the U.S. economy. Estimates of undocumented immigrant workers in the U.S. range from 3.5 to 6 million, with the vast majority from Mexico, followed by the Central American and Caribbean countries. While many are driven here by economic poverty, the vast increase in immigrants from El Salvador and Guatemala over the past few years reflects the escalation of violence in those countries. In the long run, the refugee flow can be reduced only through a solution to the current conflicts in the region and support for genuine development projects.

While working towards these goals, the United States should also implement the following:[17]

1. The Immigration and Naturalization Service (INS) should grant extended voluntary departure status to undocumented Salvadorans and Guatemalans residing in the United States. Furthermore, they should be granted permission to work and to become part of the legal labor force. Barring that, Congress should enact the DeConcini–Moakley bill, suspending the deportation of Salvadorans.

2. Political asylum should be granted to persons fleeing political persecution in El Salvador, Guatemala and Honduras, many of whom have received sanctuary from churches in the United States. The practice of requiring asylum applicants to prove they will be persecuted if they go back to their country of origin should be eliminated and a standard of proof consistent with the UN and US Refugee Acts' definition of asylum should be required (i.e. a well-founded *fear* of persecution).

3. The INS should not rely on the Department of State for information on refugee cases. As much as possible, where human rights concerns are part of the decision, up-to-date information from such sources as Amnesty International and the United Nations High Commission for Refugees should be required.

4. Legalization should be granted to Haitian refugees now in the United States.

5. The Administration should cease fomenting anti-refugee hysteria through references to "hordes of Central American refugees" who will be forced to flee their homelands if revolutionary movements are victorious. Instead, the U.S. government should take measures to create a climate in which refugees will be accepted and efforts made to resolve the problems they face as refugees in this country.

Most important, the United States should use its influences to diminish, rather than expand, war in the region, and to alleviate poverty, for these are the greatest stimuli of the refugee flow to the United States.

Notes

1. In this April 27 speech to Congress, President Reagan denied that his administration was attempting to overthrow the Nicaraguan government. "Our purpose," he declared, "in conformity with American and international law, is to prevent the flow of arms to El Salvador, Honduras, Guatemala and Costa Rica."

   In a May 4 press conference, however, the president called the anti-Sandinista guerrillas "freedom fighters," whose purpose is to restore the revolution that the Sandinistas had betrayed. See *Washington Post*, May 5, 1983. And, in a July 21 press conference, a reporter asked the president, "Do you think if this present [Sandinista] faction remains in power there cannot be a satisfactory settlement" of conflicts in the region? The president answered: "I think it'd be extremely difficult because I think they are being subverted or they're being directed by outside forces." See *New York Times*, July 22, 1983. If the recovery of the Nicaraguan revolution's true spirit is the *contras'* goal and regional stability is impossible until the current Nicaraguan government is removed, then arms interdiction doesn't seem to be the covert operation's real purpose.

   The distinction between arms interdiction and overthrowing the Nicaraguan government is lost on anti-Sandinista rebels whom the United States is funding, arming, training and supplying. In an interview published on December 9, 1982, Enrique Bermudez, commander of the Nicaraguan Democratic Forces (FDN), told the *New York Times*: "It is not acceptable to us to carry out missions to interdict Cuban and Russian supply lines to El Salvador. We are Nicaraguans and our objective is to overthrow the Communists and install a democratic government in our country." See *New York Times*, December 9, 1982. On the previous day, the U.S. House of Representatives passed, with the administration's support, the so-called "Boland Amendment," which restricted the United States from providing "military equipment, military training or advice, or other support for military activities for the purpose of overthrowing the government of Nicaragua or provoking a military exchange between Nicaragua and Honduras." See *New York Times*, December 9, 1982

2. For a discussion of the Reagan Administration's economic war against Nicaragua, see John Cavanagh and Joy Hackel, "Nicaragua: Making the Economy Scream," *Economic and Political Weekly*, November 5-12, 1983. According to the article's authors, the United States is waging an economic war against Nicaragua that parallels the Nixon Administration's economic sanctions against Chile which contributed to the coup which overthrew the democratically elected government of leftist president Salvador Allende.

   Nicaraguans estimate that U.S. pressure has deprived them of $354 million in lost trade and loans in 1983, while U.S. pressure internationally has resulted in a loss of $112.5 million in multilateral loans since 1980.

   In addition, anti-Sandinista paramilitary forces supported by the United States inflicted damage on Nicaragua's productive apparatus and infrastructure amounting to $130 million in 1982, equal to over six percent of the country's gross national product. The authors note that damage on an equivalent scale to the U.S. economy would surpass $92 million, roughly the amount that the U.S. federal government spends yearly on health and education combined.

3. According to the Department of State, between July 1979 and December 1983, Nicaragua received $175 to $200 million in military aid from the Soviet Union, and $50 to $70 million from Cuba, East Germany, Czechoslovakia, Poland, Bulgaria, North Korea and Vietnam. (Telephone interview, U.S. Department of State, January 19, 1984).

, 4. On October 20, 1983, Nicaraguan Foreign Minister Miguel D'Escoto submitted to the Reagan Administration a package of four binding accords under which the Nicaraguan government would pledge to stop the flow of arms traffic across their territory to the Salvadoran guerrillas if the United States would stop supporting anti-Sandinista rebels based in Honduras and Costa Rica. The proposed accords also would permit on-site inspections of Nicaragua and its neighbors and provide for fines and international legal penalties against any country violating the terms of the agreement. See *Washington Post*, October 21, 1983.

5. The Salvadoran armed forces number 36,150, according to the Department of State. (Telephone interview, U.S. Department of State, September 29, 1983). Between 1980 and 1983, El Salvador received $205.4 million in military aid from the United States.

   According to the Department of State, armed guerrilla forces in El Salvador now number 5,000 to 7,000. In addition, there are 4,000 to 5,000 militia who are "part-time fighters or individuals providing logistical support." (Telephone interview, U.S. Department of State, January 20, 1984). No reliable estimate is available on the value of their weapons. But sources quoted by Eldon Kenworthy say that 40 percent of the military equipment the United States gives the Salvadoran army passes to the FMLN. See Eldon Kenworthy, "Central America: Beyond the Credibility Trap," *World Policy Journal*, Fall 1983, p. 189.

6. Between October 1979 and September 1983, the Salvadoran armed forces and right-wing death squads killed more than 37,000 Salvadorans. See Americas Watch. "Human Rights Update on Central America," Washington, D.C.: Americas Watch, October 1983. p. 3.

7. U.S. military aid to Honduras has increased over 900 percent in the last four years, from $4.0 million in 1980 to $37.3 million in 1983.

8. See Lawyers' Committee for International Human Rights, Americas Watch, Washington Office on Latin America, "Honduras on the Brink: A Human Rights Report," New York: Americas Watch, February 1984; Washington Office on Latin America. "Honduras: Military Boomerang," Special Update, Washington, D.C.: Washington Office on Latin America, January 1984.

9. Amnesty International, "Guatemala: A Government Program of Political Murder," London: Amnesty International, 1981. p. 3.

10. *Ibid.*, p. 3.

11. Press Release, Amnesty International/USA, Washington, D.C., October 12, 1982. For further discussion see the Americas Watch reports: "Human Rights in Guatemala: No Neutrals Allowed," November 1982; "Creating a Desolation and Calling it Peace: May 1983 Supplement to the Report on Human Rights in Guatemala," May 1983; and "Guatemala: A Nation of Prisoners," January 1984.

12. See Wayne Smith, "Myopic Diplomacy," *Foreign Policy*, No. 48, Fall 1982.

13. See Doug Hellinger and Steve Hellinger, "Supporting Central American and Caribbean Development: A Critique of the Caribbean Basin Initiative and an Alternative Regional Assistance Plan." Washington, D.C.: The Development Group for Alternative Policies, August 1983.

14. Eligible articles are defined as:

    a. Those with over 50 percent local content and produced by businesses with at least 50 percent local ownership;

    b. Those goods produced under working conditions that meet with ILO standards;

    c. Those that for their increased production for export do not require the expanded use of critical resources, particularly land, essential to meet food needs of the local population; and

    d. Those who have not had a net negative impact on the environment in the process of their production.

15. Considerable support is gathering among labor, human rights and development organizations to amend trade legislation so that duty-free access to U.S. markets is restricted to those countries which respect internationally accepted fair labor standards.

16. For an elaboration of STABEX, see Katharina Focke, *From Lome 1 Towards Lome 2: Texts of the report and resolution adopted on 26 September 1980 by the ACP-EEC Consultative Assembly* (Luxembourg, November 1980), pp. 22–29.

17. These recommendations draw heavily upon: Norma Chinchilla and Nora Hamilton, "Working Paper on Central American Migration to the United States," paper prepared for PACCA, October 1983.

Epilogue

A Response to the Report of the National Bipartisan Commission on Central America

"You come here speaking of Latin America, but this is not important. Nothing important can come from the South. History has never been produced in the South. The axis of history starts in Moscow, goes to Bonn, crosses over to Washington, and then goes to Tokyo. What happens in the South is of no importance."

Henry Kissinger to Gabriel Valdes,
Foreign Minister of Chile, June 1969

The Commission's Recommendations

On January 11, 1984, the National Bipartisan Commission on Central America released its report. The 132 page document, prepared by a twelve-member commission chaired by former Secretary of State Henry Kissinger, charts a policy course to deal with the unrest and instability of the region.

The Kissinger Report acknowledges that the violent upheavals in Central America are rooted in poverty and repression: "Discontents are real, and for much of the population conditions of life are miserable; just as Nicaragua was ripe for revolution, so the conditions that invite revolution are present elsewhere in the region as well." But the Report

charges—with an argument built on assertion rather than evidence—
that the Soviet Union is the manipulator of indigenous revolution in the
region. "The Soviet–Cuban threat is real," the Report emphasizes,
because "the conditions which invite revolution...have been exploited
by hostile forces."[1]

The prescriptions flow directly from this misplaced diagnosis. The
Kissinger Commission recommends a $400 million "emergency stabiliza-
tion program," substantial increases in military assistance to El Salvador,
Honduras, and even Guatemala, as well as implicitly condoning a
continuation of the "covert" war against Nicaragua, which the Report
euphemistically terms an "incentive" for negotiation. To attack the root
causes of revolution and thwart future Soviet machinations, the Report
proposes an $8 billion five-year aid program with unprecedented U.S.
involvement in and responsibility for the economies of Central America.

The Commission's recommendations are alarming in two regards.
First, the military prescriptions would lead to a deepening of U.S.
military involvement in a widening war in Central America. Second, the
economic prescriptions would serve narrow private interests in the
United States at a heavy cost to U.S. taxpayers as a whole. All historical
evidence would suggest that the recommended economic aid program,
managed by the current elites in power, would have a negative impact on
the great majority of the people in Central America and would not serve
the long-term interests of U.S. citizens either. Moreover, as the widespread negative response to the Kissinger Report indicates, adherence to
its recommended course will increase political division in the United
States.

Prescriptions for Disaster

The Commission understands that development cannot occur without
peace, which it seeks through military escalation. The Kissinger Report's
primary military recommendations, however, commit U.S. military
power and prestige to unachievable objectives. The Commission proposes
that continued military aid to El Salvador be conditioned on certification
that human rights are not being violated by the government. Dr.
Kissinger dissented for the same reason that President Reagan gave in
vetoing the certification process: If the United States has a security
interest in preventing a victory of the guerrilla forces, it does not matter
what the beleaguered government does. But the diplomatic and political

costs for the United States of giving unqualified support to a regime that, according to the Catholic Diocese in San Salvador, has slaughtered 37,000 civilians in the last four years, are unacceptable. Thus, the Commission seeks to solve the dilemma by offering a third way out which simply does not exist.

U.S. diplomats have lectured, cajoled, even threatened the Salvadoran military about their murderous behavior, but most of those in charge of fighting have no interest in changing because the more they kill, the less they will have to compromise. Only through terror can the extreme right hope to retain their power. Dependent on the United States as they are, they know that the Administration, having made prevention of revolution in El Salvador a prime national security objective, is equally dependent on them. Since these U.S. clients have neither an interest in respecting human rights nor a fear that the United States will abandon them, the certification requirement is window dressing. The true recommendation of the Report, issued at a moment of major military setbacks for the government forces in El Salvador, is renewed commitment to military escalation. This comes at a moment when morale of government troops in El Salvador is collapsing.

The assertion of a national security interest in El Salvador leads logically to an increase in U.S. military commitments, should such be necessary to prevent victory by the guerrillas. Since the FDR–FMLN are becoming more effective as a military and political force and the government less so, the United States will soon be confronted with the decision whether or not to intervene with more U.S. military personnel. The thrust of the Report would appear to favor escalation, but the tragic implications and costs of committing American young men to a prolonged and bloody guerrilla war in El Salvador are nowhere spelled out. Thus, the Commission proposes a military task that cannot be achieved, except at unacceptable cost. To assert a vital interest and be unable or unwilling to defend it militarily—as the Vietnam experience demonstrated—is a recipe for eroding national power and credibility. The Commission extends this bankrupt posture beyond El Salvador to Honduras and even Guatemala.

By not clearly condemning the secret war against Nicaragua, the Commission lent its voice to the continuation of that war. Aware that more than 10,000 "contras" financed by the United States are attacking Nicaragua, the Commissioners evidently believe that military pressure either will cause the Nicaraguan government to change its internal policy in "desirable" directions, or will cause the overthrow of the Sandinistas.

Neither is likely.

As one of the Commissioners, Mayor Henry Cisneros of San Antonio, indicated in his dissent, the attempt to support domestic opposition by enlisting it in covert operations backfires. The government has little incentive to negotiate and compromise with domestic political forces that are perceived as acting in concert with a hostile foreign power in the region, particularly when that power seems committed to its very overthrow.

The Nicaraguan Revolution faces domestic opposition, but there is nothing to suggest that a military force operating from Honduras and Costa Rica can overthrow a government that retains wide popular support and national legitimacy. In more than three years of attacks, the "contras" have been unable to occupy and hold any Nicaraguan territory. The Sandinista government has armed a large part of its population and apparently can rely on it to fight forces that are viewed as agents of the United States committed to restoration of the old order. U.S. tax coffers are supporting a campaign of terrorism, murder and sabotage. Regrettably, the Kissinger Commission did not identify what vital interests of the United States are served by these activities which the Administration subsidizes but cannot acknowledge because they violate our laws, ideals and values.

Ironically, no coherent argument is presented for the assumption that the revolutions represent a threat to U.S. national security. Lacking in evidence and analysis, the Report's case is reduced to the assertion that there is a "Soviet–Cuban thrust to make Central America part of their geostrategic challenge" to the United States.[2] As Senator Daniel Moynihan suggested, this is a "doctrinal position," divorced from reality.[3] The Nicaraguan government has stated that it will not accept a Soviet base (nor has the Soviet Union indicated any interest in bearing the economic burdens necessary to gain one). Having struggled for national independence, it is inconceivable that post-revolutionary governments would elect to become Soviet bases, particularly since their economies are highly dependent upon Western aid and trade. The Soviets do not need a missile base in Central America and are not likely to risk exploring whether the United States will permit one.

The Report makes much of a domino theory that suggests that revolutions spread like communicable diseases. Ideas and examples do travel. It is hard to understand why the United States should be opposed to the spread of models that work, such as health and literacy programs, no matter who develops them. U.S. influence in the region depends not on quarantining ideas and programs of other countries, but on demonstrating a genuine interest in development and democracy in the region, rather than viewing the countries as so many pawns in a geopolitical chess game. It is noteworthy that the principal "dominoes" of the region for whose sake the security policy is ostensibly pursued—Mexico and Panama—oppose the military course of U.S. policy in Central America. The Commission Report eschews analysis, however, relying on reiteration of a Communist peril: "No nation is immune from terrorism and the threat of armed revolution supported by Moscow and Havana."[4] "Such extreme language," as Senator Edward Kennedy commented, "raises the stakes of the contest to such a level that anything short of total military victory becomes unthinkable."

The Commission's economic program calls for two new economic institutions and for U.S. entry into a third that already exists. A new Central American Development Organization (CADO) would be created to supervise the allocation of about a quarter of U.S. bilateral economic assistance to the region. A new Central American Development Corporation would promote and finance privately-owned projects. The United States would join the Central American Bank for Economic Integration (CABEI) which finances public and private economic projects in Central America.

Behind a shield of stepped-up military aid, the United States would take direct responsibility for organizing the economies, societies and cultures of the region. U.S. personnel would train Central America's teachers, doctors and police. Experts from the United States would design the region's land and urban reform programs; U.S. union organizers would guide Central American unions; U.S. political scientists would carve Central American democratic institutions. A U.S. representative, armed with veto power over $2 billion worth of aid, would "negotiate" with representatives of the region's recipient countries on the conditions for getting the money. The program is suffused with prevailing U.S. economic and political ideology. The emphasis is on free markets, with a heavy role for private enterprise, especially U.S. corporations. These new institutions would reinforce the strong influence over Central American economic development which the United States already exercises through its commanding position in the International Monetary Fund, the World Bank Group, the Inter-American Development Bank, and various bilateral aid and loan guarantee programs.

The Commission has thus proposed a program of U.S. responsibility for the battered economies of Central America that is unprecedented in the post-World War II era. The plan smacks more of the British East India Company than the Marshall Plan. The post-war Marshall Plan for Europe also had a political objective, but its success was due to its emphasis on eliciting regional initiative and planning. The local energies, institutions, experience and political will were all in place. U.S. money and ideas served as the catalyst. In Central America, the U.S. role is not that of catalyst, but of re-organizer of chaos and repression. Even if our geopolitical motives for undertaking this enormously expensive commitment were not so clearly revealed, such an intrusive role in the internal affairs of the region would be bitterly resented and would feed the very nationalist currents which the Administration is trying to contain.

The history of the last generation suggests why the North-americanization of Central America is doomed to failure. In 1961, the United States attempted to counter the appeal of the Cuban revolution by offering Latin America the Alliance for Progress, an $18 billion initiative for peaceful reform. As the Commission Report admits, the Alliance helped to stimulate growth in Central America, but failed to produce either structural economic change or political reform. Since the aid was not targeted at basic human needs, it only served to widen the gap between rich and poor. Moreover, the extensive military and police operations designed to provide the "shield" for the development program strengthened the most vigorous enemies of democracy and reform in the hemisphere. By the late 1970s, the growth came to an end, inequality had worsened, and much of the hemisphere was ruled by U.S.-backed military dictators.

The Commission's recommendations repeat the same error. To implement equitable development would require removal of elites who have no interest in reducing their privilege. Yet the military thrust of the Commission's policy is designed to bolster those very elites in El Salvador and Guatemala, and to undermine Nicaragua, one of the few countries in the region that has a leadership interested in redistribution of wealth and power.

Fundamental redistribution will succeed only if there is popular participation rather than elite domination of the decision-making process. This is a vital aspect the Kissinger Commission neglected both in its whirlwind fact-finding visit to the region and in its published report. Finally, the ultimate formulation of any sensible solution for the region cannot come from ideas imposed from outsiders, but instead must be rooted in Central Americans' own experience and interpretation of their history, something the Kissinger Report only superficially addresses.

Conclusion

The Kissinger Commission's Report proceeds from a commendable statement of principles to a disastrous recommendation of policies. Many of the princples it espouses, such as self-determination, concern for human rights, support for democracy, are those which inform PACCA's *Changing Course: Blueprint for Peace in Central America and the Caribbean.* How is it possible that the same principles can lead to such widely divergent policy recommendations? The Kissinger Commission arrived at its self-defeating conclusions by ignoring history and misperceiving current reality. The result is a policy course that leads inescapably towards military escalation.

The effects of a long history of invading, subverting and dominating the nations of Central America are simply glossed over. The Report reviews this history and then cavalierly concludes:

> Perhaps the United States should have paid more attention to Central America sooner. Perhaps over the years we should have intervened less, or intervened more, or intervened differently. But all these are questions of what might have been. What confronts us now is a question of what might become.

No one wishes to dwell on mistakes of the past, but it is impossible to evaluate the Commission's own program without taking history and resulting attitudes in the region into account. Nicaraguan suspicion of U.S. policy objectives can only be understood by comprehending the U.S. role in creating and sustaining a Somoza dynasty, which the Commission labels a "kleptocracy." It would be hard to support the covert war against Nicaragua had analysis been made of the long-term consequences of the "successful" CIA operation in Guatemala. The overthrow of a nationalist reform government there in 1954 has produced a legacy of repression and horror and a generation of internal war.

The Kissinger Commission ignores the legacy of past U.S. actions and compounds its consequences by advocating more of the same. In the face of overwhelming evidence to the contrary, the Commission asserts that the governments of El Salvador and Guatemala are reformable, that the powerful in those countries will support structural economic reform and democratization. At the same time, the U.S. interest is defined as requiring unremitting hostility to Nicaragua. To conclude, as the Commission does, that "of the nations in the region, only the Sandinista leadership in Nicaragua...has been ambiguous about—if not hostile to—open, multi-party political contests..."[7] is caricature, not serious analysis. The Commission could not be unaware of the jailed, maimed, murdered opposition leaders in Honduras, Guatemala and El Salvador, and the grotesque record of "free" elections in those countries.

Time is running out for the United States in Central America. By constructing an elaborate rationale for intensifying policies that cannot work, the Kissinger Commission has failed an historic challenge. The citizenry and the Congress must act to change our course before it is too late.

Notes

1. *Report of the National Bipartisan Commission on Central America*, January 1984, p. 4.
2. *Ibid.*, p. 12.
3. *New York Times*, January 13, 1984.
4. *Report of the National Bipartisan Commission on Central America*, January 1984, p. 14.
5. *Washington Post*, January 15, 1984.
6. *Report of the National Bipartisan Commission on Central America*, January 1984, p. 2.
7. *Ibid.*, p. 7.

Appendix I

U.S. Economic Interests in the Region

All U.S. economic activity falls into one of four categories: corporate investment and subcontracting, trade, private financial involvement, and bilateral and multilateral aid.

Corporate Investment and Subcontracting

U.S. direct investment in Central America and the Caribbean (minus the Netherlands Antilles) totalled $20.8 billion in 1981, or 9.2 percent of total U.S. investment abroad.[1] (Close to three-fifths of the region's total consisted of financial investment concentrated in a few countries which serve as tax havens). U.S. corporations have around 1,400 subsidiaries in Central America[2] and over 1,700 in the Caribbean,[3] including 70 of the largest 100 U.S. corporations. Cheap labor is the basic attraction to investment in the region, which is concentrated in petroleum refining, light industry, and food production and processing. A corporate official whose firm operates in St. Kitts said: "They work more minutes per hour" at 10 percent higher labor productivity than in the United States and at wages one-tenth those in the United States.[4]

Since the onset of global economic recession in 1979, new direct investment into the region has slowed while another form of transnational corporate involvement has spread. Through what is known as international subcontracting, medium and large U.S. corporations contract the most labor intensive phases of automobile, semiconductor, apparel, toy, and other assembly industries to Central American and

Caribbean workshops. In these locales, predominantly female laborers perform sewing, piecing together and other forms of tedious assembly work. Once assembled, the goods return to the United States with duty paid only on the value added abroad. Such forms of subcontracting account for over half of industrial exports to the United States from most of the region's countries. In the cases of Haiti, El Salvador, Costa Rica and Barbados, over three-quarters of their industrial exports to the United States are subcontracted goods.[5]

Since the conditions and types of U.S. investment and subcontracting vary widely in the region, it is difficult to generalize about their impact. Corporations benefit from generous incentives, cheap labor, low transport costs and high profits. At the same time, foreign investment often produces goods for local markets and, under the right conditions, can be beneficial for economic development. Contrary to assertions by the U.S. government, Nicaragua, for example, believes that most foreign investment can be beneficial and has passed one of the most open foreign investment codes in the region.

Trade

A sizable share of a few commodities imported into the United States comes from the region: bauxite (85 percent); bananas (69 percent); sugar (17 percent); coffee (15 percent); and beef (14 percent).[6] When the subcontracted manufactured goods and other imports are added to these figures, U.S. imports from Central America and the Caribbean totalled $8.6 billion in 1982, about 3.4 percent of total U.S. imports. U.S. exports to the region totalled $6.7 billion, or 3.2 percent of the U.S. total.[7]

Even more important from a strategic angle, nearly half of U.S. foreign trade, including petroleum, passes through the Panama Canal and the Caribbean Sea. Except for the U.S. blockade of Cuba in the early 1960s, no nation has ever posed a threat to the free flow of goods in the area, and large quantities of goods can be expected to flow unimpeded to and through the region in the future.

Private Financial Flows

Even more than transnational corporations, private banks have become involved in the region, both through loans and through offshore banking centers in the Caribbean. By the middle of 1982, the external public debt of the region's countries approached $23 billion.[8] While this amounts only to about 8 percent of the debt owed by Latin America as a whole, it includes several Caribbean Basin nations which have defaulted or come close to defaulting on repayments, and which have entered into austerity programs with the International Monetary Fund (including Costa Rica, Honduras, El Salvador, Panama and Jamaica).

U.S. private bank exposure in the region totalled $2.3 billion by the end of 1982, as against $3.1 billion by banks from other countries.[9] Political pressure has played a role in lending practices. In the wake of a major 1980 rescheduling of $560 million of Nicaragua's external debt, the U.S. government urged U.S. banks to cut the country off. Despite an implicit promise by U.S. private banks that new loans would be forthcoming, only $11 million has flowed to Nicaragua following the rescheduling.[10]

A more realistic picture of the U.S. banks' stake in the region emerges when bank transfers to offshore banking centers are added to the total. The centers attract banking business by reducing or eliminating taxes and other levies and restrictions on operations, and have flourished in the Bahamas, the Cayman Islands, the Netherlands Antilles and Panama. In 1982, U.S. bank exposure in these havens totalled $22.8 billion.[11]

As with investment, bank loans have proven to be a mixed blessing. While transnational banks have earned record profits from Latin American loans, Central American and Caribbean nations ran up record debts over the past decade, whose repayment has drained scarce foreign exchange away from development projects. Still, it remains the sovereign right of any nation to decide whether and on what terms it wishes to incur external indebtedness. Such flows can, again under controlled conditions, contribute to development, and a U.S. government policy which ties the flow to political conditions can only distort the development process.

Bilateral and Multilateral Aid

Over the past two decades, U.S. foreign economic assistance has flowed through four channels: multilateral institutions (about 14 percent), bilateral development assistance (33 percent), bilateral P.L. 480 "Food for Peace" (20 percent), and bilateral security supporting assistance (now known as the Economic Support Fund) excluding military (33 percent).[12] For fiscal year 1983, the Administration has proposed outlays of $7 billion in economic assistance, about a tenth of which will flow to Latin America (about half of the bilateral total for Latin America goes to Central America: $323 million in 1983).[13] The Caribbean and Central American share shot up by $350 million during the first year of the Caribbean Basin Initiative.

Whereas aid allocations under President Carter were (at least on paper) subject to recipients' fulfillment of certain human rights criteria, President Reagan shifted the criteria. He has used economic aid to buttress military and security objectives, and has reversed a long-term trend away from bilateral toward multilateral aid. A case in point is the Combination Action Program launched in El Salvador in 1983. Modelled after a program implemented by the United States during the Vietnam war, the program combines military sweeps against insurgents with economic assistance in war-torn provinces in the countryside.[14]

In similar fashion, the Reagan administration has used bilateral and multilateral institutions in waging economic war against Nicaragua. By April 1981, all U.S. bilateral aid to the country was severed, while an embargo was placed on previously authorized P.L. 480 food credits for the purchase of wheat. Government programs that promote U.S. foreign investment, such as Export-Import Bank guarantees and Overseas Private Investment Corporation assistance, were halted. Extending the economic straitjacket to trade, Reagan rescinded 90 percent of Nicaragua's longstanding quota to sell sugar on U.S. markets.[15] Each action contradicted the Reagan administration's stated goal of promoting free trade and private investment in the Third World.

Reagan further spread the economic campaign into institutions mandated to remain apolitical—the multilateral lending organizations. In 1983, Reagan officially ordered the U.S. representatives to the World Bank and Inter-American Development Bank to vote against any loans to Nicaragua, a formalization of what had already become unofficial policy.[16]

Instead of trying to meet the basic needs of the region's population, government economic aid has increasingly become a direct arm of U.S. national security policy.

Notes

1. Calculated from Obie G. Whichard, "U.S. Direct Investment Abroad in 1982," *Survey of Current Business*, August 1983, p. 23. The Netherlands Antilles were excluded from the figures because billions of dollars show up in U.S. corporate affiliates there to escape U.S. withholding taxes on interest payments to foreigners. Of the $20.8 billion total, $4.8 billion was in Central America, and $16.0 billion was in the Caribbean.

2. The Resource Center, *Dollars and Dictators: A Guide to Central America* (Albuquerque: The Resource Center, 1982), p. 8.

3. Figures supplied by the Resource Center in Albuquerque, New Mexico, in December 1983.

4. Marc Herold and Nicholas Kozlov, "Autos and Chemicals versus Bras and Calculators: Genuine Capitalist Industrialization versus a Parable of Trends," paper prepared for PACCA, October 1983, p. 34.

5. Computed from data in United States, International Trade Commission, *Imports Under Items 806.30 and 807.00 of the Tariff Schedules of the United States, 1977–1980*. Publication 1170. Washington, D.C.: USITC, July, 1981; U.S. Department of Commerce, Bureau of Census. *Highlights of U.S. Export and Import Trade*. FT990. Washington, D.C.: USDOC, December 1982; and computer data sheets of the U.S. International Trade Commission, August 1983.

6. Figures from the U.S. Department of Agriculture (for 1981), quoted in The Resource Center, *Dollars and Dictators, op. cit.*, p. 10.

7. Calculated from data in *Highlights of U.S. Export and Import Trade, op. cit.*, pp. 32, 72.

8. Estimated by INIES/CRIES, quoted in Mark Hansen, "U.S. Banks in the Caribbean: Towards a Strategy for Facilitating Lending to Nations Pursuing Alternative Models of Development," paper prepared for PACCA, October 1983, p. 4.

9. Figures from the Bank for International Settlements, quoted in *Ibid.*, p. 5.

10. *Financial Times*, September 5, 1983.

11. Hansen, *op. cit.*, Table 3.

12. Richard S. Newfarmer, "U.S. Foreign Economic Policy Toward Latin America," (unpublished manuscript prepared for the Overseas Development Council, Washington, D.C., January 1983), p. 7.

13. *Ibid.*, p. 8; and Washington Office on Latin America, "U.S. Assistance to Latin America: Profound Reorientations." Occasional Paper #2. Washington, D.C.: Washington Office on Latin America, May 1982, pp. 2-3.

14. David Landes, "Bilateral Economic Aid Policy," paper prepared for PACCA, October 1983, pp. 1-2.

15. Reagan cut Nicaragua's quota of 59,000 tons of sugar exports to the United States for fiscal year 1983 to 6,000 tons, a reduction equalling $15 million in export earnings.

16. Jim Morrell and Jesse Biddle, "Central America: The Financial War," paper prepared for PACCA, October 1983, pp. 6-11.

Appendix II

Profiles of Countries in Central America[1] and the Caribbean[2]

Guatemala

POPULATION: 7.1 million (most populous in Central America)
AREA: 42,000 square miles (about the size of Kentucky)
ECONOMY: depends on coffee, banana, cotton exports
ILLITERACY: 60 percent
PER CAPITA INCOME: U.S. $1,198

Guatemala has historically been the most economically powerful nation in Central America, but half the population average only $81 income each year. This half are the pure-blooded Indians (descendants of the great Mayans) who are among the poorest and most isolated people in the hemisphere. In the late seventies the Indians suddenly began to form revolutionary bands. They and other exploited Guatemalans became the targets of a 20,000-man army trained and largely supplied by the United States. That army runs the government, and it is a direct descendent of a regime placed in power by a U.S.-planned *golpe* (or coup) in 1954 that overthrew the constitutionally elected, reformist Arbenz government. In 1980 a U.S. official surveyed the spreading revolution, and the government's response of massacres and torture, then observed: "What we'd give to have an Arbenz now."

Honduras

POPULATION: 3.7 million (slightly less than Louisiana's)
AREA: 43,000 square miles (about the size of Louisiana)
ECONOMY: depends on banana and coffee exports
ILLITERACY: at least 60 percent
PER CAPITA INCOME: U.S. $640

The original "banana republic," Honduras has become the closest ally of the United States in the region while remaining the poorest and most undeveloped state in the hemisphere other than Haiti. U.S. fruit companies controlled the country after 1900. In the sixties, they were joined by New York and California based banks (Citicorp, Chase Manhattan, Bank of America) that took over the financial system. Life expectancy of adults is forty-nine years; more than 20,000 families live on the edge of starvation; and in rural areas families of ten to twelve children are not uncommon, although half die before the age of five. Because it is the only Central American country with boundaries on three of the other four nations, Honduras has traditionally served as a base for revolutionaries and counterrevolutionaries—thus the United States used it as a staging area to overthrow the Guatemalan government in 1954 and to "destabilize" the Nicaraguan government in the early eighties. Although civilians sometimes occupied the presidency after 1945, the country has mostly been ruled by military officers trained and equipped by the United States. The country's dire poverty has been caused partly by foreign exploitation, partly by rampant internal corruption, and partly by sterile mountainous terrain. A Honduran legislator once crumpled a sheet of paper, dropped it on his desk, then observed, "That is an outline map of Honduras."

El Salvador

POPULATION: 4.75 million (most densely populated in region)
AREA: 8,236 square miles (the size of Massachusetts)
ECONOMY: depends on coffee exports and U.S. aid
ILLITERACY: at least 50 percent
PER CAPITA INCOME: U.S. $680

Its name is sometimes translated as "Saviour of the World," but its people are among the world's five worst-fed populations. One reason: At least half of all Salvadorans depend on the land for a living, but fewer than 2 percent (the "oligarchs" or "Fourteen Families") control nearly all the fertile soil and 60 percent of all the land. With a 3.5 percent rate of population increase (one of the world's highest), the demands on the soil have become so great that erosion is ruining the land area and extinguishing entire species of indigenous animals and plants. After a 1979 *golpe*, the army—trained and supplied by the United States—seized some of the Fourteen Families' power, but that power was only diminished, not destroyed. Stereotyped as the hardest workers in the region (the "Germans of Central America," the phrase goes), many Salvadorans historically have had to emigrate to survive. Since the revolution accelerated in the late seventies, one-tenth of the population, or about 300,000 people, have entered the United States illegally for refuge. They had reasons other than economic for doing so: During 1980 and 1981 the military and right-wing terrorists killed approximately 30,000 civilians to stop spreading revolution. Such a bloodbath (equivalent to killing more than two million of the U.S. population) is not new; fifty years earlier, the military killed a similar number of peasants for similar reasons.

Nicaragua

POPULATION: 2.7 million (most thinly populated in region)
AREA: 57,000 square miles (about the same as North Carolina)
ECONOMY: depends on coffee, sugar, cotton, timber exports
ILLITERACY: 60 to 70 percent before 1979 revolution
PER CAPITA INCOME: U.S. $897

Modern Nicaragua, that is to say the revolution that seized power in mid-1979, was shaped by U.S. military occupation (1911–33), and then the U.S.-created and supported Somoza family dynasty (1934–79). That family seized most of the wealth, including a land area equal to the size of Massachusetts. Meanwhile 200,000 peasants had no land. The major causes of death were gastrointestinal and parasitic diseases, and infant maladies. The country played a pivotal role in Washington's diplomacy because of the Somozas' willingness to act as U.S. instruments, and also because natural waterways made it a possible site for an interoceanic canal. Its significance greatly increased after the Sandinist revolutionaries seized power in 1979. No regime in the world cooperated more fully with the United States than did the Somozas between 1930 and late seventies, and no Central American nation has more directly challenged U.S. policies in the area than the post-1979 Nicaraguan government.

Costa Rica

POPULATION: 2.5 million (one of the most rapidly increasing in the world)
AREA: 20,000 square miles (smaller than Arkansas)
ECONOMY: depends on coffee, banana, sugar exports
ILLITERACY: low, probably less than 10 percent
PER CAPITA INCOME: U.S. $1520

The most democratic, equitable, and literate Central American nation, Costa Rica was oddly blessed by poverty. Christopher Columbus called it "Rich Coast" (Costa Rica) because the Indians wore gold jewelry, but it actually had no minerals and so European adventurers lost interest in it. Instead, industrious Spaniards drove out the Indians, developed farms, and thus established a widely held land base for the strongest and longest-lasting democratic system in Latin America. Unlike the population of the other four countries, Indians are few in number. People of Spanish ancestry control the power centers. After the 1948 revolution, the government outlawed the army, although a U.S.-trained national police of 5,000 efficiently maintains order. Stability and climate made the country a favorite retirement spot for North Americans. But the hemisphere's highest birthrate, combined with oil and price inflation and a steep decline in coffee export prices, caused the most severe crisis in thirty years during the early eighties. Possible cuts in the nation's extensive social welfare system threatened to open Costa Rica to the political upheavals that already ripped apart the other Central American nations.

Western Caribbean

The islands of the western Caribbean, also known as the Greater Antilles, include Cuba, Hispaniola (comprised of Haiti and the Dominican Republic), Jamaica and Puerto Rico.

These countries were colonized in the 1700s, and witnessed a gradual extermination of their native peoples and a rise of slave plantations with labor brought from Africa. While slavery was abolished between the early and late 19th century, beginning with the Toussaint L'Ouverture revolt in Haiti in 1802, tremendous social inequality still remains. With the exception of Cuba, the western Caribbean countries remain under the strong economic and political domination of the United States.

Dominican Republic

POPULATION: 5.5 milion (1981)
AREA: 18,919 square miles
PER CAPITA INCOME: $1,260 (1981)
EXPORTS: $704 million (1980); sugar accounts for $307 million, 44 percent of
     total

The Dominican Republic is perhaps best known for having surrendered large tracts of its land to the sugar subsidiary of one of the United States' largest multinationals, Gulf & Western. This and other multinationals have enjoyed decades of almost uninterrupted "stable" dictatorship. Upon the assassination of Rafael Trujillo in 1961 (dictator since 1930), landed oligarchs and others with financial interests tried unsuccessfully to establish a new political order. In 1963, Juan Bosch, representative of the newly formed Dominican Revolutionary Party (PRD) was elected by a popular vote. After seven months, the army ousted him, which caused a mass uprising among his supporters— workers, students, poor and unemployed. This movement overpowered the military-oligarch alliance until the invasion of 22,000 U.S. marines in April of 1965. Joaquin Balaguer, Trujillo's right hand man, was installed as President.

Since then, the Dominican Republic has survived a series of failed economic policies and two elections, which put power in the hands of Antonio Guzman in 1979 and Salvador Jorge Blanco in 1981. Excessive borrowing over the past decade has led the Dominican Republic down the familiar road to debt-induced austerity programs.

Haiti

POPULATION: 5.5 million (1981)
AREA: 10,811 square miles

PER CAPITA INCOME: $300 (1981)

EXPORTS: $197 million (1980); coffee accounts for $91 million, 46 percent of
total

This former French colony, in which French creole is still spoken,
became independent in 1802 as a result of a slave revolt. It was the first
Caribbean island to break free of slavery, and it became the first black
independent nation in the Western hemisphere.

Haitians, however, have suffered slavery of another sort under the
dictatorships of the Duvalier family. Francois "Papa Doc" Duvalier was
elected president in 1957 and was succeeded by his son, Jean-Claude
"Baby Doc" Duvalier, who has declared himself president for life. The
family lives in an enclave of luxury on an island of squalor.

Haiti is the poorest and least developed country in the Americas.
Extreme repression and unemployment have caused thousands to flee
the country over the past years. Some 40,000 Haitians each year depend
for their survival on cutting cane in the Dominican Republic.

Cheap labor and other tax incentives have made Haiti attractive to
transnational corporations, and provided assembly line jobs for Haitians
migrating to the capital from the countryside. Since the best farmland is
used for export crops, there is very little food production on the island.
Haiti must rely on food imports, usually too expensive for the average
Haitian to buy.

Cuba

POPULATION: 9.9 million (1981)

AREA: 44,401 square miles

PER CAPITA INCOME: $1,400 (1979)

EXPORTS: $5.5 billion (1980); sugar accounts for $4.6 billion, 84 percent of total

Following Cuba's independence from Spain in 1898, the United States
maintained extensive economic and foreign policy control over the island
until 1959, when revolutionaries, led by Fidel Castro, overthrew the
U.S.-supported Batista dictatorship.

Despite U.S. threats, attempted assassinations, economic blockades
and the missile confrontation of 1961, the Cuban revolution, still under
the leadership of Castro, has completed its first quarter century. It
receives its major economic support from the Soviet Union, much of it

through barter arrangements rather than in hard cash. Cuba also trades with capitalist countries, which supply 40 percent of its imports and provide a market for about 15 percent of its exports.

Jamaica

POPULATION: 2.2 million (1981)
AREA: 4,247 square miles
PER CAPITA INCOME: $1,180 (1981)
EXPORTS: $942 million; bauxite and alumina account for $737 million, 78
percent of total

Aside from a flourishing underground marijuana crop, sugar cane is Jamaica's traditional export crop. In recent years, however, minerals have taken over as the leading export. Although Jamaica is the world's third largest producer of bauxite, production and export declined dramatically in 1982. The country has also depended heavily on tourism, which, following a decline in the late 1970s, due in part to political violence, has been on the upswing since 1981.

In 1972, the People's National Party (PNP), led by Michael Manley, won state power on the platform of democratic socialism. IMF austerity programs, however, placed constraints on Manley's socialist policies. Economic chaos prevailed and his party lost in 1980 to Edward Seaga (Jamaican Labor Party), a Reagan favorite, who has attempted to make Jamaica attractive to foreign investors.

Puerto Rico

POPULATION: 3.2 million (1981)
AREA: 3,436 square miles
PER CAPITA INCOME: $3,000 (1980)
ECONOMY: depends on United States transfer payments

A Spanish colony until the United States invaded in 1898, Puerto Rico remains a U.S. Commonwealth. Although Puerto Ricans are U.S. citizens, the country has no U.S. congressional representation and the United States determines its defense and foreign policy.

During the first three decades of this century, U.S. investors appropriated large tracts of land for sugar and tobacco, eliminating land which could have been used for domestic food production. By 1928, food imports already amounted to a third of all imports to the island.

In the wake of the Great Depression, a new political party led by Luis Muñoz Marin was formed on the platform of independence and anticorporatism. This party, the Popular Democratic Party (PPD), was in power from 1940–68, but after World War II, which was a boom for the Puerto Rican economy, the party abandoned its original platform and returned to an economic policy based on foreign corporate investment in export industries. This policy, which became known in the 1950s as "Operation Bootstrap," failed to increase employment or develop Puerto Rico, leaving the island even more dependent on U.S. aid.

Presently, Puerto Rico's economy remains dominated by U.S. multinationals (particularly the pharmaceutical industry), while the U.S. government continues to provide transfer payments (i.e. food stamps) to meet the basic material needs of the people. Puerto Rico imports more U.S. products per capita than any country in the world.

Eastern Caribbean

The Eastern Caribbean (the Lesser Antilles) includes the islands of Barbados, Dominica, Grenada, Guadeloupe, Martinique, St. Lucia, St. Vincent, Trinidad and Tobago and the Netherlands Antilles. Together they form an arc of more than 2,000 km extending from the east of Puerto Rico to the Venezuelan coast. The tiny islands have, on average, a surface area of about 400 square kilometers, with the exception of Guadeloupe and Martinique, which are over 1000 square kilometers each, and Trinidad and Tobago, which is 5000 square kilometers. Colonized by the British, French, Spanish and Dutch, much of the area was turned into sugar plantations worked by slaves.

Since World War II, the British island-colonies have become independent states, dependent upon international aid. The French colonies of Guadeloupe and Martinique retain the status of "overseas provinces" and, thanks to French transfer payments and social benefits, maintain a higher standard of living than their neighbors.

The countries of the Eastern Caribbean have a combined Gross Domestic Product of $9 billion, $5 billion of which originates from Trinidad and Tobago's large petroleum industry. Guadeloupe and Martinique account for almost $3 billion of the area's GDP, while the other countries combined generate another $1 billion.

With the exception of Trinidad and Tobago, the Eastern Caribbean countries depend primarily on agricultural exports (sugar, bananas, cocoa, coconuts) and tourist industries. Total revenue from exports hovers around $4.5 billion (1980 statistics), with the lion's share ($3.9 billion) from Trinidad and Tobago.

Barbados

POPULATION: 250,000 (1981)
AREA: 166 square miles
PER CAPITA INCOME: $2,200 (1981)
EXPORTS: $150 million (1980); sugar accounts for $58 million, 34 percent of
total

Barbados, independent from Britain since 1966, has governed itself constitutionally since 1885. The re-election of the Barbados Labor Party to its second five-year term in 1981 coincides with serious economic problems brought about by a severe decline in all sectors of the economy. Sugar cane output was lower in 1981 than at any time since 1948. Both the tourist industry (the largest single employer) and the manufacturing sectors have been hard hit by the global recession. Manufacturing (mainly electronic components and garments) is composed chiefly of offshore assembly plants established by U.S. corporations to take advantage of comparatively cheap labor and tax incentives.

Dominica

POPULATION: 80,000 (1981)
AREA: 289 square miles
PER CAPITA INCOME: $620 (1981)
EXPORTS: $7.4 million (1980); fruit and nuts account for $3.2 million, 43
percent of total

Independent from Britain since 1978, Dominica has endured corrupt political leadership (the first Prime Minister, Patrick John, tried to sell the entire north of Dominica to a U.S. company later exposed to be working for South Africa), as well as the destruction of 60 percent of Dominica's main export crops and much of its infrastructure following

Hurricane David's 1979 sweep across the island. After squandering most of the reconstruction aid, and losing U.S. support, the government lost power in a 1981 election to the right-wing Dominican Freedom Party led by Eugenia Charles.

Grenada

POPULATION: 111,000 (1981)
AREA: 289 square miles
PER CAPITA INCOME: $625 (1981)
EXPORTS: $16.9 million (1980); cocoa accounts for $6.8 million, 40 percent of
total; spices, $4.0 million, 23 percent of total

Grenada was granted independence from Great Britain in 1974. Following five years of rule by the corrupt, unpopular Sir Eric Gairy, the New Jewel Movement took power in a coup led by Maurice Bishop. The movement's priority was the social welfare of the majority of Grenadans, and it succeeded in bringing education, improved health care, roads, etc. to the previously impoverished population. Bishop's admiration for Fidel Castro, along with a Cuban labor force on the island, incurred U.S. hostility. The focal point of this opposition was construction of an international airport that Bishop claimed was necessary for tourism, but which the United States claimed was a potential Soviet landing strip.

Tensions within the New Jewel Movement erupted into violence in October 1983 when Bishop and several allies were murdered. The upheaval provided a pretext for the October 25 U.S. invasion.

Martinique

POPULATION: 340,000 (1981)
AREA: 425 square miles
PER CAPITA INCOME: $4,650 (1980)
EXPORTS: $117 million (1980); refined petroleum products account for $53
million, 45 percent of total

Guadeloupe

POPULATION: 325,000 (1981)
AREA: 687 square miles
PER CAPITA INCOME: $3,850 (1980)

EXPORTS: $107 million (1980); sugar accounting for $44 million, 41 percent of
total

For both countries, tourism is the fastest growing industry, but it is not
enough to absorb rising unemployment from the stagnating agricultural
sector. Labor costs on Martinique and Guadeloupe are about five times
higher than elsewhere in the region, making their prices for bananas and
sugar less competitive on world markets.

As French overseas provinces, the islands have enjoyed a higher
standard of living than their Caribbean neighbors, despite their internal
economic problems. In recent years, however, French austerity programs
have reduced assistance and other benefits.

St. Lucia

POPULATION: 120,000 (1981)
AREA: 239 square miles
PER CAPITA INCOME: $630 (1978)
EXPORTS: $33.7 million (1980); fruit and nuts account for $10.8 million, 32
percent of total

Since independence from Britain in 1967, St. Lucia enjoyed a decade of
steady growth until a combination of the cumulative effects of
government mismanagement, a decline in tourism, and Hurricane Allen
(August 1980) threw the country into steep economic decline. The
newly elected (1982) United Workers Party under the leadership of John
Compton is rebuilding the manufacturing sector (flour milling, footware,
and electronic industry assembly) destroyed by the hurricane. Tax
incentives have encouraged foreign investment, aiding the industrial
reconstruction.

St. Vincent

POPULATION: 116,000 (1981)
AREA: 131 square miles
PER CAPITA INCOME: $380 (1978)
EXPORTS: $15 million (1979); fruits and nuts

St. Vincent is comprised of Bequia, Mustique, Mayreau, Canouan, and
Union Islands in the Grenandines, as well as the larger island of St.

Vincent. While the conservative government's policies have been successful in reactivating the industrial and agricultural sectors following the 1979 eruption of Volcano Soufriere, the maintenance of an offshore banking sector, and proposals to sell or lease the island of Canouan to an unidentified foreign consortium for development into a major tourist and financial enclave has met with criticism from the left-wing opposition party.

Trinidad and Tobago

POPULATION: 1.1 million (1981)
AREA: 1,930 square miles
PER CAPITA INCOME: $5,670 (1981)
EXPORTS: $4.1 billion (1980); petroleum accounts for $3.8 billion, 92 percent of
total

Trinidad and Tobago is the wealthiest of the Eastern Caribbean countries due to its own oil reserves, and because it maintains huge refineries which process a portion of Venezuela's oil exports. The islands, which gained their independence from Britain in 1962, had primarily a sugar-producing, agriculture-based economy until the the exploitation of new oil fields and the subsequent increase in the price of oil. The petroleum industry, however, has not been able to overcome the unemployment problem created by the decline in agricultural sectors.

Netherlands Antilles

POPULATION: 250,000 (1981)
AREA: 386 square miles
PER CAPITA INCOME: $3,150 (1978)
EXPORTS: $5.3 billion (1980); petroleum accounts for $4.8 billion, 90 percent of
total

The Netherlands Antilles consists of six islands off the Venezuelan coast: Aruba, Bonaire, and Curacao (the Leewards); and to the north: St. Maarten, St. Eustatius, and Saba (the Windwards). The islands have been in Dutch possession since 1634. Granted autonomy but not yet independent (the Netherlands controls their defense and foreign policy), they serve as both important oil refining centers and tax havens for transnational banks.

South American Caribbean

In the northeastern-most region of South America, Suriname, Guyana, and French Guiana share a coastline which faces the Caribbean. Stretching over some 12,000 km, these three countries have a combined population of about 1.2 million. The region was bypassed by the Spanish during the colonial era because of its sparse population; but the British, Dutch, and French soon filled in the geopolitical vacuum. The British introduced slaves from Africa, India and Asia; the Dutch brought in Indonesians, Indians, Chinese and Africans; and the French imported Africans and Chinese.

The regional economy is based largely on exports to the United States: bauxite from Guyana and Suriname, and fish from French Guiana.

Suriname

POPULATION: 350,000 (1981)
AREA: 62,934 square miles
PER CAPITA INCOME: $2,350 (1978)
EXPORTS: $495 million (1980); bauxite and alumina account for $353 million,
        71 percent of total

Suriname is the only Latin American country (and one of 10 countries in the world) with a fully integrated aluminum industry (e.g. the mining of bauxite as well as the production of alumina and aluminum). This industry accounts for a fifth of GDP and a third of government revenues. Agriculturally, Suriname is self-sufficient in rice, and produces bananas, shrimp, palm oil and other commodities for export.

Guyana

POPULATION: 795,000 (1980)
AREA: 83,011 square miles
PER CAPITA INCOME: $680 (1980)

EXPORTS: $290 million (1980); bauxite accounts for $129 million, 45 percent of total

The economic evolution of Guyana has been dominated by the decline in bauxite production (output decreased from 4.5 million tonnes in 1970 to 2 million in 1981) and the fall in the price of sugar, the country's second major export product. The bauxite mines were nationalized in 1971 as part of the country's attempt to chart an independent economic policy. President Forbes Burnham has banned the import of many foodstuffs in hopes that the shortages will force people to favor locally grown and manufactured products. The country is self-sufficient in rice, but there is a flourishing black market for other food imports.

French Guiana

POPULATION: 63,000 (1981)
AREA: 35,135 square miles
PER CAPITA INCOME: $2,850 (1981)
EXPORTS: $25 million (1980); fish accounts for $9 million, 38 percent of total

French Guiana, a French overseas territory, is almost totally dependent upon France for its economic development. Though most of its exports are destined for the United States and Japan, France supplies two-thirds of its imports. French Guiana is also the French space and satellite launching center.

Notes

1. Copyright 1983 Walter LaFeber. Reprinted by permission of the publisher, W.W. Norton, 500 Fifth Avenue, New York, NY, 10110, from *Inevitable Revolutions.* The book is available from your local bookstore.
2. These profiles were drawn from data in: Enver Carim, ed., *Latin America & Caribbean, 1983* (Essex: World of Information, 1983); Pete Ayrton, ed., *World View 1983* (New York: Pantheon, 1982); United Nations, *United Nations Conference on Trade and Development Statistics.* (New York: United Nations, 1983); Fred Halliday, "Cold War in the Caribbean," *New Left Review,* September–October, 1983; and other trade sources.

Appendix III

PACCA Position Papers

National Security and Related Policy Issues

Robert Borosage, William LeoGrande, Saul Landau, and Richard Barnet, "National Security Argument on Central America."

Phil Berryman, "The Case for Accommodation: United States Policy Toward Central American Revolutions."

Saul Landau, "Inside Nicaragua's Class War."

Philip Brenner, "The Cuban Question."

Edward L. King, "U.S. Military Policy in Central America."

Economic Policy

Robert Armstrong, "Dollars and Doctrines: U.S. Economic and Political Interests in the Caribbean Basin."

Jim Morrell and Jesse Biddle, "Central America: The Financial War."

David Landes, "Bilateral Economic Aid Policy."

John Cavanagh and Joy Hackel, "Multinational Corporations in Central America and the Caribbean."

Marc W. Herold and Nicholas Kozlov, "Autos and Chemicals versus Bras and Calculators: Genuine Capitalist Industrialisation versus a Parable of Trends."

Mark E. Hansen, "U.S. Banks in the Caribbean Basin: Towards a Strategy for Facilitating Lending to Nations Pursuing Alternative Models of Development."

John Weeks, "Economic Crisis in Central America."

Richard S. Newfarmer, "U.S. Foreign Economic Policy Toward Latin America."

Social Policy Issues

Roxanne Dunbar Ortiz, "The Indian Question in Central America."

Norma Chinchilla and Nora Hamilton, "Working Paper on Central American Migration to the United States."

PACCA
2288 Fulton, #103
Berkeley, CA 94704

Appendix IV

U.S. Security Assistance and Economic Aid to Central America, 1979-1985

Note: Figures represent millions of dollars.

U.S. financial assistance through government corporations such as the Overseas Private Investment Corporation (OPIC) and the Commodity Credit Corporation (CCC) is not included.

In its Fiscal Year 1984 supplemental request, the Reagan administration asked for $2 million in unspecified Peace Corps funds for the Caribbean region.

Abbreviations

AID—Agency for International Development

ESF—Economic Support Fund. Officially classified as a "security assistance" program, the ESF provides grants and loans "to promote economic and political stability in countries and regions where the United States has special security or foreign policy objectives," according to an AID document. See *Washington Post*, November 4, 1983. The monies finance projects such as the construction of bridges and roads. They are also used to address emergency needs—for food, medical supplies, or balance of payments support.

FMS—Foreign Military Sales financing program

IMET—International Military Education and Training

MAP—Military Assistance Program

PL480—Public Law 480 (Food for Peace program)

Sec.506 grants—Emergency powers granted to the President under Section 506 of the Foreign Assistance Act to provide military assistance in case of "an unforeseen emergency."

Costa Rica	FY 1979	FY 1980	FY 1981	FY 1982	FY 1983	FY 1984 Continuing Resolution	FY 1984 Supplemental Request	FY 1984 Total	FY 1985 Request
Total U.S. Aid	**17.9**	**15.5**	**15.0**	**54.4**	**218.1**	**109.2**	**82.9**	**192.1**	**219.9**
Total U.S. Security Assistance	—	—	—	**22.1**	**161.6**	**72.2**	**67.9**	**140.1**	**170.0**
MAP	—	—	—	2.0	4.5	2.0	7.9	9.9	9.8
FMS	—	—	—	—	—	—	—	—	—
IMET	—	—	—	.1	.1	.2	—	.2	.2
Sec. 506 grants	—	—	—	—	—	—	—	—	—
ESF	—	—	—	20.0	157.0	70.0	60.0	130.0	160.0
Total U.S. Economic Aid	**17.9**	**15.5**	**15.0**	**32.3**	**56.5**	**37.0**	**15.0**	**52.0**	**49.9**
AID	16.4	13.6	11.5	11.5	27.1	15.1	8.0	23.1	20.0
Peace Corps	1.5	1.5	1.7	1.7	1.7	1.9	—	1.9	1.9
PL 480 Title I	—	—	—	18.0	27.5	20.0	7.0	27.0	28.0
PL 480 Title II	—	.4	1.8	1.1	.2	—	—	—	—

El Salvador	FY 1979	FY 1980	FY 1981	FY 1982	FY 1983	FY 1984 Continuing Resolution	FY 1984 Supplemental Request	FY 1984 Total	FY 1985 Request
Total U.S. Aid	**11.4**	**65.2**	**139.5**	**268.2**	**326.8**	**259.7**	**316.4**	**576.1**	**473.6**
Total U.S. Security Assistance	—	**15.1**	**80.4**	**197.0**	**221.3**	**184.8**	**268.7**	**453.5**	**342.5**
MAP	—	5.7	10.0	8.5	33.5	45.0	178.7	223.7	116.0
FMS	—	.3	.5	16.5	46.5	18.5	—	18.5	15.0
IMET	—	—	—	2.0	1.3	1.3	—	1.3	1.5
Sec. 506 grants	—	—	25.0	55.0	—	—	—	—	—
ESF	—	9.1	44.9	115.0	140.0	120.0	90.0	210.0	210.0
Total U.S. Economic Aid	**11.4**	**50.1**	**59.1**	**71.2**	**105.5**	**74.9**	**47.7**	**122.6**	**131.1**
AID	6.9	43.2	32.8	36.2	58.8	41.3	30.0	71.3	80.0
Peace Corps	1.6	.6	—	—	—	—	—	—	—
PL 480 Title I	—	3.0	17.2	27.3	39.0	32.0	14.0	46.0	44.0
PL 480 Title II	2.9	3.3	9.1	7.7	7.7	1.6	3.7	5.3	7.1

Guatemala	FY 1979	FY 1980	FY 1981	FY 1982	FY 1983	FY 1984 Continuing Resolution	FY 1984 Supplemental Request	FY 1984 Total	FY 1985 Request
Total U.S. Aid	**24.7**	**13.4**	**18.8**	**25.2**	**19.6**	**15.9**	**20.0**	**35.9**	**108.9**
Total U.S. Security Assistance	—	—	—	**10.0**	—	—	—	—	**45.3**
MAP	—	—	—	—	—	—	—	—	—
FMS	—	—	—	—	—	—	—	—	10.0
IMET	—	—	—	—	—	—	—	—	.3
Sec. 506 grants	—	—	—	—	—	—	—	—	—
ESF	—	—	—	10.0	—	—	—	—	35.0
Total U.S. Economic Aid	**24.7**	**13.4**	**18.8**	**15.2**	**19.6**	**15.9**	**20.0**	**35.9**	**63.6**
AID	17.4	7.8	9.1	7.9	12.2	1.6	20.0	21.6	40.0
Peace Corps	2.0	1.9	2.1	1.7	2.0	2.3	—	2.3	2.3
PL 480 Title I	—	—	—	—	—	7.0	—	7.0	16.0
PL 480 Title II	5.3	3.7	7.6	5.6	5.4	5.0	—	5.0	5.3

Nicaragua	FY 1979	FY 1980	FY 1981	FY 1982	FY 1983	FY 1984 Continuing Resolution	FY 1984 Supplemental Request	FY 1984 Total	FY 1985 Request
Total U.S. Aid	**16.9**	**37.1**	**59.7**	**6.2**	—	—	—	—	—
Total U.S. Security Assistance	**8.0**	**1.1**	**56.6**	**5.1**	—	—	—	—	—
MAP	—	—	—	—	—	—	—	—	—
FMS	—	—	—	—	—	—	—	—	—
IMET	—	—	—	—	—	—	—	—	—
Sec. 506 grants	—	—	—	—	—	—	—	—	—
ESF	8.0	1.1	56.6	5.1	—	—	—	—	—
Total U.S. Economic Aid	**8.9**	**36.0**	**3.1**	**1.1**	—	—	—	—	—
AID	1.7	18.3	1.8	.7	—	—	—	—	—
Peace Corps	.2	.1	.1	—	—	—	—	—	—
PL 480 Title I	2.6	15.0	—	—	—	—	—	—	—
PL 480 Title II	4.4	2.6	1.2	.4	—	—	—	—	—

Honduras	FY 1979	FY 1980	FY 1981	FY 1982	FY 1983	FY 1984 Continuing Resolution	FY 1984 Supplemental Request	FY 1984 Total	FY 1985 Request
Total U.S. Aid	**31.2**	**56.5**	**47.5**	**112.0**	**143.2**	**127.6**	**123.5**	**251.1**	**204.8**
Total U.S. Security Assistance	**2.3**	**3.9**	**8.9**	**68.1**	**93.3***	**81.0**	**110.0**	**191.0**	**137.5**
MAP	—	—	—	11.0	27.5	40.0	37.5	77.5	61.3
FMS	2.0	3.5	8.4	19.0	9.0	—	—	—	—
IMET	.3	.4	.5	1.3	.8	1.0	—	1.0	1.2
Sec. 506 grants	—	—	—	—	—	—	—	—	—
ESF	—	—	—	36.8	56.0	40.0	72.5	112.5	75.0
Total U.S. Economic Aid	**28.9**	**52.6**	**38.6**	**43.9**	**49.9**	**46.6**	**13.5**	**60.1**	**67.3**
AID	22.0	45.8	25.7	31.2	31.2	31.8	8.0	39.8	45.0
Peace Corps	2.1	2.0	2.4	2.6	3.2	3.7	—	3.7	3.4
PL 480 Title I	2.0	2.0	5.8	7.0	10.0	8.0	4.0	12.0	15.0
PL 480 Title II	2.8	2.8	4.7	3.1	5.5	3.1	1.5	4.6	3.9

*This figure does not include funds to finance the joint U.S.-Honduran military maneuvers that were conducted in Honduras during 1983, nor does it include monies for the U.S.-sponsored construction of airstrips, a hospital, and other military facilities in Honduras that coincided with the maneuvers. In its FY84 and FY85 budget requests, the Reagan administration has asked for a total of $45 million for the Regional Military Training Center (RMTC), which was established in Honduras in 1983 for the "low-cost, large-scale" training of Salvadoran and Honduran troops.

Sources

Center for International Policy, *Central America: The Financial War*, International Policy Report, Washington, D.C.: Center for International Policy, March, 1983, p. 8.

U.S. Department of Defense, Defense Security Assistance Agency, *Foreign Military Sales, Foreign Military Construction Sales and Military Assistance Facts as of September 1982*. (Washington, D.C.: Data Management Division, DSAA, 1983).

U.S. Department of State, *Country Reports on Human Rights Practices* (Washington, D.C.: U.S. Government Printing Office, 1980).

U.S. Department of State, *Country Reports on Human Rights Practices for 1983* (Washington, D.C.: U.S. Government Printing Office, 1984).

U.S. Agency for International Development, "Congressional Presentation, Fiscal Year 1985 (mimeo), Annex III, Latin America and the Caribbean, Volume III.

U.S. Department of State, "Briefing Book: Central America Democracy, Peace and Development Initiative" (mimeo), February, 1984.